Pesos or Plastic?

Ken Mitchell · Robert H. Scott, III

Pesos or Plastic?

Financial Inclusion, Taxation, and Development in South America

palgrave
macmillan

Ken Mitchell
Department of Political Science
and Sociology
Monmouth University
West Long Branch, NJ, USA

Robert H. Scott, III
Department of Economics, Finance
and Real Estate
Monmouth University
West Long Branch, NJ, USA

ISBN 978-3-030-14875-1 ISBN 978-3-030-14876-8 (eBook)
https://doi.org/10.1007/978-3-030-14876-8

Library of Congress Control Number: 2019933317

This Palgrave Pivot imprint is published by the registered company Springer Nature Switzerland AG
The registered company address is: Gewerbestrasse 11, 6330 Cham, Switzerland

To Brielle, Ava, Alex and Luli

Acknowledgements

This book would not have been possible without the generous support of Monmouth University. The authors wish to thank Steve Pressman, Phil Howard and Sam Maynard for comments on early drafts of Chapters 2 and 3—of course, all mistakes and errors are the sole responsibility of the authors. Tula Weis and Ruth Noble, at Palgrave, shepherded this project from start to finish and the authors extend their sincere appreciation for overseeing an efficient and organized publication process.

Contents

List of Figures

List of Tables

Introduction

Public revenue and how to mobilize more of it stand as a pivotal economic and political challenge across South America, and this book provides a new, unorthodox framework for doing so in the coming decades. Policy-makers can only break the cycles of economic stagnation, commodity dependence, poverty and inequality once they possess sufficient public resources. Development on the cheap is a myth and magic policy bullets devised by ideological conservatives and progressives continue to fail and cause hardship. Since the Second World War, South America's tax-to-GDP only tops Africa and lags far behind industrialized countries. The great divide between developed and developing nations is in their capacity to collect tax revenue and how it is spent. South America must address the problem of low tax revenue in a meaningful way in order to climb the development ladder in the twenty-first century. The evolution of taxation in the region has led every country to adopt a national value-added tax (VAT)—i.e., indirect tax on consumption. Consumption is the largest component of Gross Domestic Product (GDP), so taxing it broadens the tax base. Today, VAT is the largest source of tax revenue across South America. As economic globalization deepens and puts pressure to cut taxes on personal and corporate income, and as South American countries continue to shift from industrial to service economies, the reliance on VAT will grow. In sum, the region's future economic development is tethered to governments crafting new strategies to raise VAT efficiency.

Taxing consumption has not by itself solved the problem of low tax revenue in South America. Because national VAT systems incorporate millions of daily consumer transactions for goods (food or clothes) and services (medical or psychoanalysis sessions), evasion through various methods is common. As a result, actual tax revenue remains well below potential tax revenue. New developments in technology, however, have simplified tracking consumption. In addition, as electronic payments became more common over the last fifteen years, VAT compliance rates increased. Even small improvements in VAT compliance can translate into significant tax revenue gains. Perhaps equally important, these gains are not temporary; they are lasting since payment method choice is often consistent. Orthodox analysts argue that VAT is a regressive tax since the poor and the rich consumers who pay endure the same tax burden. But, of course, whether VAT is regressive or progressive depends on how governments utilize or allocate collected VAT revenue. We argue throughout this book that VAT could, in fact, be progressive. How? With a broad and stable tax base, South American governments could adopt European VAT norms and institutions, which is to say earmarking VAT revenue for a modern social welfare state that benefits the poor and society in general (education, health care and public infrastructure).

The findings in this book provide sufficient evidence that South American countries can create elevated and more stable public revenue. And improving tax collections will not require drastic changes to public institutions in the form of bureaucratic reforms, cultural shifts nor increases in tax rates. Likewise, we anticipate that the unrelenting global pressure to cut personal and corporate income taxes will continue. Using existing systems, increasing tax revenue is a matter of improving consumption tax compliance, which is best done by encouraging more consumers to use electronic payment methods rather than cash. Once revenue grows, these countries can earmark these revenue gains to advance a progressive development agenda that combats poverty, lowers inequality and improves living standards across South America.

This book comprises three substantive chapters and a brief conclusion. Chapter 1 is a broad historical overview of VAT in South America. We explain when and how VAT began in South America to its current level of dominance. We also discuss the history of financial inclusion in general and microcredit in particular, and how the former has changed in the past two decades. We find that microcredit has produced no strong empirical evidence that it alleviates poverty or promotes development.

In many cases, microcredit seems to result in people getting poorer due to burdensome debt obligations that are all too often predatory. This was not what economist Muhamad Yunus envisioned when he founded the Grameen Bank; but it has evolved from neoliberal pro-market poverty killer to another way for some shady lenders to make money off disadvantaged people. However, we reconceptualize financial inclusion to be people having bank accounts and using them (i.e., active users). As financial inclusion has grown, VAT has risen and the informal or shadow markets have shrunk. The shrinking of the informal markets is critical since it filters down many levels—it shows a change in consumer behavior and a resilient one so far and emphasizes that change is possible without a cultural lobotomy or what the tax literature refers to as tax morale.

Chapter 2 is a case study of Argentina looking at how the country went from having the lowest tax-to-GDP among middle-income countries worldwide to fifteen years later being tied with Brazil as the highest tax-to-GDP countries in the region. Argentina is now a higher tax revenue country, something regional experts failed to anticipate. This rapid and dramatic increase in tax revenue is the source of several factors. We explain in this chapter how it came about and why it is historic and a meaningful example of how to improve government finances without major structural changes. We develop several time series regressions that test the relationship between VAT-to-GDP in Argentina and increases in credit card use, debit card use, cash use, bank participation and total credit card spending to total consumption. And the results are illuminating.

Chapter 3 compares the taxes, change in credit card, debit card and cash use in Argentina, Brazil and Chile. The goal is to inquire whether the experience of Argentina crosses over to its neighbors. We look at how VAT revenue changed in all three countries as financial inclusion (as measured by bank account usage) increased—leading to increases in card use and a decline in cash. Using a series of fixed-effects regressions, we find that the increases in VAT are correlated with rising financial inclusion and of particular importance, a reduction in the size of the informal economy across all three countries.

The final chapter concludes the book with a brief synopsis and analysis of what our research findings mean for economic development in South America and similar regions worldwide. The shift to consumption taxes is a global rather than a regional phenomenon. Essentially, high and stable tax revenues create the opportunity for greater economic stability, but equally important, it creates the opportunity for governments to provide people with the social programs and benefits that will reduce poverty and inequality and promote the development of human capital and infrastructure that ushers in greater prosperity across the region.

CHAPTER 1

Financial Inclusion and the Middle of the Pyramid, a New Public Revenue Strategy for the Twenty-First Century

Abstract This chapter begins with a recognition that developing economies collect less in tax revenue than developed economies, and this presents obstacles to economic and political modernization. Low tax revenue is a chronic problem in Latin America, where regional tax-to-GDP lags behind the OECD average—in 2016, the gap stood at 22.7–34.3% (OECD 2018). Low tax revenue stunts industrialization, causes de-industrialization, worsens commodity dependency, undermines public infrastructure, retards educational and health systems, encourages high poverty, inequality and crime, and ensures periodic economic crises. Recent decades saw a shift in public finances to dependency on Value Added Tax (VAT) revenue: in 2016, VAT accounted for 29.3% of Latin American tax revenue, the region's largest revenue stream, more than personal income, corporate, trade or property taxes (OECD 2018). This chapter explores why this shift occurred, constraints on VAT collection linked to sizable informal or shadow ("non-taxed") economies, and how government policies in the area of financial inclusion together with consumer behavioral shifts can improve VAT evasion rates in the future.

Keywords Taxation · Economic development · South America · Financial inclusion · Microcredit · Conditional cash transfers

K. Mitchell and R. H. Scott, III, *Pesos or Plastic?*,
https://doi.org/10.1007/978-3-030-14876-8_1

Introduction

Margaret Levi starts *Of Rule and Revenue*, her seminal work on the political economy of taxation, by linking the modern state's evolution to its capacity to tax and stresses "[a]t the foundation of increases in a state's provision of goods and services is its revenue production systems" (Levi 1988: 1). No developed tax system, no developed state (Kaldor 1963; Migdal 1988; Tilly 1990; Steinmo 1993; Brautigam et al. 2008; Bahl and Bird 2008; Fuest and Zodrow 2013; Besley and Persson 2013). Goods and services imply more than the standard public healthcare, education and infrastructure, and includes enforcement of property rights and other essential regulatory activities modern states perform in order to chart a Northian path to economic and political development (see Huntington 1968; North and Thomas 1973; North 1990; Bates 2001; Besley and Persson 2009; Acemoglu and Robinson 2012). Underdeveloped states collect insufficient tax revenue and the result fosters the conditions for protracted economic and political stagnation and cyclical financial crises, due to the fact that such states must either abdicate from essential tasks, print too much domestic currency, or borrow unsustainable sums from abroad.[1]

Diagnosing ills, especially those developing states encounter, is easy enough, but conventional solutions to the problem eluded above (i.e., insufficient tax revenue) have a poor track record. Neoliberals call for fewer "public goods and services" and lower overall rates of taxation designed to boost economic growth in the private marketplace—more economic growth, more taxation. But this approach runs into two problems. First, unregulated markets rarely deliver as promised and too often, the product is a large informal market, less secure property rights, and substitution of public for private monopolies. Informal markets are, by and large, a product of ineffective or nonexistent regulation tied to low state capacity—for example, the average size of the shadow economy as a percentage of the total economy from 1991 to 2015 in the USA (8.34%) and Germany (11.97%) fell well below Brazil (37.63%) and

[1] In 2018, we saw all three on display in South America: abdication in the form of modern slavery and illegal mining and logging across large swaths of the interior of Brazil, out-of-control printing of currency in Venezuela (80,000% inflation rate), and reckless foreign borrowing in Argentina ($57 billion from IMF).

Argentina (24.14%) (Medina and Schneider 2017).[2] Informal markets skirt taxes, thus reducing tax revenue, and become the bane of economic development, contrary to neoliberal advocates (de Soto 1989). Second, political constraints intercede. Free people as well as newly economically mobile people (Lipset 1959; Huntington 1968) demand more not fewer state goods and services, a reality witnessed in developed and developing countries. On the other hand, statists assume away the existence of a weak state unable to collect tax and jump to supplying more goods and services, and either borrow or print currency to stimulate the economy. Neither neoliberal nor statist approaches furnish a sustainable solution to the pivotal issue: how to collect enough and consistent tax revenue for the modern state's requisite institutional development? Or, as Besley and Persson (2013) sum up the challenge of development, "[h]ow does a government go from raising around 10% of GDP in taxes to raising around 40%?" This book presents an alternative approach to both questions that adheres to the existing political, economic and institutional constraints found in three South American countries (Argentina, Brazil and Chile).

Financial crises have become commonplace in South America. In the last few decades, inflation, high unemployment, currency devaluations, debt accumulation, low aggregate demand and so on have plagued the region intermittently.[3] In 2018, the regional landscape included Venezuela's 80,000% annual inflation rate (highest in the world) and 15% annual GDP decline, Argentina's 48% annual inflation rate

[2]Different definitions exist for the shadow, informal, black or underground economy, but our main focus is on VAT revenue, its collection and its avoidance and Sung et al. (2017: 6) is a useful place to start: "[T]he shadow economy defined from the perspective of taxation comprises two types of activities: (i) activities of unregistered informal enterprises (including individuals) operating completely outside the formal economy (undeclared work, UW), and (ii) activities of register companies in the formal sector intentionally underreporting their sales (underreporting, or UR)."

[3]In South America, sovereign defaults since 1960 include Argentina (1982, 1988, 2001, and 2005), Brazil (1961, 1964, 1983, 1986, and 1990), Chile (1961, 1963, 1966, 1972, 1974, and 1983), Ecuador (1982, 1984, 2000, and 2008), Peru (1969, 1976, 1978, 1980, and 1984), Uruguay (1983, 1987, and 1990), and Venezuela (1982, 1990, 1995, 1998, 2004, and 2017). Argentina and Brazil penned over 20 IMF emergency agreements each over this period—including the IMF's largest-ever country loan of $57 billion to Argentina in 2018. Countries experiencing hyperinflation since 1960 (often more than once) include Argentina, Bolivia, Brazil, Chile, Ecuador, Peru and Venezuela (currently).

(4th highest in the world), 50% currency devaluation, 26% government bond interest rate (highest in the world) plus $57 billion in emergency IMF aid (an historical high), and Brazil's 9.4% government bond interest rate (third highest in the world), rising poverty after a 7% GDP contraction (2015–2017) and a near sovereign default at the start of May. While each financial crisis is unique, several factors are often present. The final trigger of most financial crises in South America is that government debt increases to unsustainable levels causing financial markets to doubt whether debt obligations can be serviced. Financial market doubts put pressure on domestic currencies (Peso, Real, or Bolivar), and currency devaluation with national debts largely in US dollars makes a default, or an emergency IMF bailout, all but inevitable.

Government debt is largely the result of two important related factors: first, the government trying to stimulate the economy through fiscal policy (i.e., increasing government spending to compensate for lower consumer spending). When a government has spent too far beyond their means, it has often led to double-digit (or more) inflation. Rising inflation creates economic uncertainty and a loss of faith in a president, a ruling party or a central banker, thus adding more instability. Second, as a consequence (or perhaps cause) of an economic slowdown, tax revenue shrinks, which puts more pressure on the government to deficit spend. These two factors are not mutually exclusive. In fact, as an economy slows tax revenues decline, which entices the government into more deficit spending (or draconian austerity policies that cut spending at the worst time exacerbating the problems). Sometimes a government's interventions can stabilize a shrinking economy. But, as we contend in this chapter (and book), it is the loss of tax revenue that puts the greatest pressure on a government to spend excessively (or cut spending) and create a downward debt spiral that is difficult to reverse. Had South America matched the OECD tax-to-GDP average in the 1980s, 1990s and 2000s, much economic and political suffering and turmoil would have been avoided. In South America, the problem of low tax revenue is particularly pernicious, which is why it shows up as a common theme across crises.

Two opposing economic realities amplify the problem of government debt accumulation in South America: (a) countries have become dependent on Value-Added Tax (VAT) revenue, and (b) countries all feature large informal (shadow) economies where it is difficult to collect VAT revenue. As inflation starts to rise or macroeconomic conditions deteriorate, a sizeable percentage of consumers and producers are incentivized to shift seamlessly between formal and informal markets. Consumers seek out lower prices in street markets. Producers, especially small and medium-sized enterprises (SMEs), undertake the rational cost/benefit decision to operate informally rather than formally. Movement into the informal economy presents an urgent problem for tax collection. As VAT has grown to provide a greater portion of tax revenue since the 1980s, any disruption in *formal* consumer spending is bound to have a corresponding effect on overall tax revenue. Here is where the end game of a debt spiral results, as an economic downturn morphs into a full-blown economic crisis. Consumption and VAT revenues fall inevitably as an economy contracts; yet, this decline is compounded by a significant percentage of remaining consumption moving from formal to informal markets.[4]

The above scenario roughly depicts regional circumstances in the 1980s and 1990s. However, an important anomaly occurred thereafter as VAT revenue grew and remained stable at elevated levels despite a slowdown in the macroeconomy. Simply put, this should not have occurred—and seasoned regional tax experts predicted that it would not occur (see Tanzi 2007; Lustig and McLeod 2009). Perhaps most dramatically, the regional economic slowdown that began around 2011 and continues into 2019 that has sapped consumer spending should have caused a significant drop in VAT revenue, as witnessed during economic down cycles in the 1980s and 1990s. But it has not. Why? Our research shows (see Chapters 2 and 3) that this reflects increasingly larger amounts of consumer spending, often regular daily spending on food and other basic household items, shifting from cash to credit cards and

[4]Common to most South American economic crises is the inevitable call from abroad to "dollarize" a local economy. Why does this issue resurface? Take the case of Argentina. Aside from the USA, it has the second largest sum of US dollars in circulation (behind only Russia). All social classes of Argentines stuff US dollars around the kitchen or bedroom. The US dollar is the currency of choice in the Argentine informal market, everything from rental properties to street venders prefer US dollars. When the macroeconomy contracts, an immediate uptick in US dollar transactions occurs and along with it pressure on the peso. Argentines have weathered economic crises each decade since the Second World War (and before), with massive crises at the start of the 1980s, 1990s, 2000s and most recently 2018. Argentine informal institutions or norms (see North 1990), both with regard to consumers and businesses, include an anticipation that actors in consumer markets will shift seamlessly in and out of formal and informal markets to maximize utility.

debit cards, a consumer behavioral change that pulls more consumption into formal and out of informal markets despite macroeconomic conditions worsening.

The influences behind consumer behavioral changes are not well understood. While a growing literature is available on financial literacy and financial inclusion, much of this work focuses on the poor (i.e., the bottom of the pyramid) and giving them access to bank accounts and money transfer technologies that are more efficient and safer than informal banking (i.e., burying money in the backyard or loan sharks). However, we find that while this may be a laudable goal, it does not explain the rise in VAT revenue, and the benefits derived from financial inclusion among the poor are unclear and may not exist with the donor community's signature financial inclusion initiatives, namely, microcredit and microfinance schemes (see discussion below).

We find evidence that the key to stable VAT revenue lies in the middle of the pyramid (i.e., the middle classes) and drawing such households into the formal banking system and inducing them to substitute traditional cash transactions for card-based transactions. Cash is king in informal markets, as Kenneth Rogoff asserts in *The Curse of Cash* (2017). We show in subsequent chapters how consumer behavioral change, notably among middle-class consumers, has shrunk the informal markets in Argentina, Brazil and Chile during times of both economic boom and economic bust. In sum, as consumption has shifted from informal (hard to tax) markets to formal (easier to tax) markets, VAT revenue has increased and shown itself to be surprisingly sticky or resilient to economic downturns. Bird and Gendron are undoubtedly correct when they say, "Almost without exception, developing and transitional countries need both more revenue and better revenue systems" (Bird and Gendron 2007: 6). Both outcomes, we maintain, are possible if governments prioritize policies of financial inclusion focused on the formal banking sector and on reducing cash consumer transactions. If South Americans continue to alter their consumer behavior toward more cards and less cash, there is reason to be optimistic about the future both with respect to resolving Levi's "modern state development and tax revenue" linkage as well as reducing the frequency of economic crises in the region.

The rest of this chapter includes the following sections. First, an overview of VAT in South America is presented that explains the history of its adoption and how it has evolved in our three case studies. Second, we discuss financial inclusion and how it has played an important role in both increasing tax revenues throughout South America and helped to reduce informal (shadow) economies. Third, we present a summary and connect this chapter to the proceeding chapters in the book.

The Value-Added Tax: *Paths to VAT Dependence in Argentina, Brazil and Chile*

Richard Bird and Pierre-Pascal Gendron open *The VAT in Developing and Transitional Countries*, arguably the most comprehensive book on the subject, by proclaiming "Few fiscal topics are more important than the value-added tax (VAT)" (Bird and Gendron 2007: 1). True, back in 2007, and more accurate today, especially in South America. VAT is the largest tax stream in most developing regions, including South America, and developing countries, including Argentina, Brazil and Chile (Dioda 2012; OECD 2018). And current trends assure greater future VAT dependency in South America—deepening of financial globalization, relentless IMF pressure to cut corporate and personal income tax, anti-tax and anti-regulatory ideology espoused by the regional hegemon (i.e., the USA), services (hardest to tax) replacing industry (easier to tax) in national economies, weak public sector institutional capacity and collapsing public trust in governments that saps tax morale (i.e., norms tied to tax evasion).

Worldwide VAT is the most common consumption tax, where "value added" means a tax on the difference between a firm's sales and its input costs. For final consumers, VAT is embedded or hidden in the final bill of sale. VAT is easiest to collect at the custom house on imported final consumer goods and at intermediate stages of production chains. The former is due to the convenience afforded tax authorities at ports and the fact that most countries operate few large commercial ports. The latter is true because for a firm to receive a VAT rebate for its inputs a VAT receipt must be submitted to the tax authorities—no receipt, no rebate. In short, stronger compliance incentives exist in firm-to-firm transactions. Firm-to-final customer transactions are harder to collect VAT (i.e., evasion is more common), especially in the areas of final consumption of domestic goods and services. High rates of evasion occur in two pivotal areas: (1) domestically produced and sold food (the largest category of household consumption) as evidenced by street markets and small informal produce businesses; and (2) individual-provided services such as doctor, lawyer, plumber, and psychoanalyst sessions. Tax authorities are ill-equipped to regulate the high volume of these transactions and both provider (psychoanalyst) and customer (patient) have an incentive to skirt VAT.

Take the example of psychoanalysis. Argentina leads the world in psychologists per capita at around 198 per 100,000 (or around 1 per every 650 Argentines), and around half reside in Buenos Aires. In regular visits to Buenos Aires since the late 1990s, the authors have yet to encounter a middle-class (or wealthier) Argentine not undergoing regular therapy sessions. People often visit multiple therapists and most children start therapy at an early age. And the industry operates in the shadow economy overwhelmingly.

Without question, how well governments reduce VAT evasion in the shadow or informal markets will be critical to public revenue generation across South America. In Argentina, Brazil and Chile, contributions to national GDP of *services* and *industry* foretell a task that will grow more urgent and difficult. Where VAT evasion is most common (services) is growing fast and where it is less common (industry) is falling. Take the most recent decade (2007–2017): Argentine industry fell (27.42–21.74%) and services grew (49.51–56.92%), Brazilian industry fell (23.13–18.48%) and services grew (57.73–63.07%) and Chilean industry fell (39.94–29.96%) and services grew (48.49–57.59%).

VAT's expansion across the globe is linked to the postwar development of the European common market, the third world debt crisis together with neoliberal structural adjustment of the 1980s, and the collapse of communism followed by multilateral-guided transitions to market economies across Eastern Europe and Central Asia of the 1990s (Bird 1992; Ebrill et al. 2001; Mahon 2004; Bird and Gendron 2007; Tanzi 2013). Europeans invented the VAT to fund post-WWII reconstruction, appearing first in France in 1948, and later to promote European common market integration as VAT replaced trade tariffs among members. VAT adoption is a requirement for common market membership; for example, the UK adopted a VAT in 1973 when it entered the common market (on the European VAT experience, see Aaron 1981; de La Feria 2009). By 1990, a total of 50 countries had a VAT and by 2018, the total surpassed 160 countries, including all OECD countries (except the USA) and all South American countries. In sum, VAT's expansion in recent decades marks the most significant trend in public finance of developing countries (Gillis 1989; Ebrill et al. 2001; Bird and Gendron 2007; Keen and Lockwood 2010).

In Europe, VAT offers at least two general advantages.[5] First, basic accounting principles call for a broad base, which consumption as the largest component of GDP provides, because it permits low rates to produce significant revenue that can stabilize public sector finances.[6] Second, linking VAT revenue to generous social welfare states cultivates political norms ("everyone contributes, everyone benefits") that over time strengthens the legitimacy of the social welfare state as well as the tax system across social class and subnational divides. European conservative governments (Merkel in Germany, Rajoy in Spain and May or Cameron in the UK) do not seek to dismantle national health systems, for example, while more progressive governments (Gentiloni or Renzi in Italy, Hollande in France, Schroder in Germany and Brown and Blair in the UK) by and large leave alone VAT revenue, even though it is more regressive than traditional income or property taxes. Norms around VAT and social welfare provision over decades help explain this outcome.

Germany is a good example. Chancellor Schroder (1998–2005) of the center-left Social Democratic Party (SDP) enacted economic reforms ("Agenda 2010") that proved pivotal to subsequent German economic growth and featured a 25% reduction in the basic rate of income tax, a slash in corporate tax from 56 to 38% but no change to the VAT rate of 16%. In 2007, Chancellor Merkel (2005–2020) of the center-right Christian Democratic Union (CDU) bumped VAT up to 19%, kept income taxes unchanged, and slashed corporate taxes further from 38% down to 29%. Perhaps Europe's most left-wing recent leader, President Hollande (2012–2017) of France, upped (slightly) VAT from 19.6 to 20%, and, after a brief and sizable income tax hike, he ended his term by cutting income tax, which left the income tax rate lower and the VAT rate higher than when he took office![7]

[5] Applying Europe's VAT experience to today's developing world is controversial. A chicken-or-egg dilemma is often overlooked, European welfare states pre-date VAT's appearance. National health insurance, for example, dates to Bismarck (1880s) in Germany while Britain's National Health Service started in 1948. This means VAT revenue funded highly popular public programs that already existed, a context that is uncommon in the developing world.

[6] In 2017, consumption as percentage of GDP for Argentina (84.34%), Brazil (84.19%) and Chile (77.57%) surpassed the totals in developed countries such as the USA (68.84%), Japan (55.69%) and Germany (53.10%).

[7] Interestingly, during the Brexit debates inside the UK, no quarter suggests that the UK outside of the EU should eliminate VAT. British norms around VAT appears strong and independent of EU membership.

Europe's consensus around VAT contrasts with the discord in the USA, the latter has no national VAT and no national consensus on provision and financing of public goods such as public pensions (i.e., Social Security) and healthcare. As recently as in 2017, the USA's congress with conservative majorities fell one vote short of ending public healthcare provision to 24 million people, a sum equivalent to the combined populations of Sweden, Norway, Denmark and Finland. Since the late 1970s, periodic VAT debates occur in the USA; yet, the two main political parties object to a national VAT and it goes nowhere.[8] Democrats decry it as regressive while Republicans fear it would generate too much revenue and permit a European-style social welfare state. Current US President Trump denounced VAT in countries that trade with the USA, calling it a plot to steal American jobs (Presidential Debate, September 26, 2016)—note that "Nearly all economists think a well-functioning VAT does not promote exports" (Slemrod 2011: 186). Countries with a national VAT tend to rebate VAT taxes on exports; for example, the German government rebates VAT on German cars exported to the USA while the German government collects VAT on USA cars imported into Germany. No country shares the USA's approach to VAT; in fact, the two countries most economically integrated with the USA, its NAFTA partners Canada and Mexico, both have a national VAT. On the other hand, the European approach now can be seen beyond Europe, with countries such as Ghana, Estonia, the Philippines and South Africa all earmarking revenue from VAT rate hikes to national health systems (Keen 2012; WHO 2017).

Brazil in 1967 became the first non-European country to adopt a national VAT, part of its 1965 constitutional reform that followed a military coup in 1964. Perhaps a European-style consensus exists in Brazil, its original VAT law was in the constitution written by military generals and its current VAT law was put in the 1988 constitution by elected officials and political parties in a context of democracy (see Longo 1994). Powerful right-wing (Cardoso 1995–2003) and left-wing (Lula 2002–2010) governments have amended the constitution but preserved VAT rates or raised them. How a regressive tax spread to South American

[8] For a recent exchange on the pros and cons of a VAT in the USA, see the debate between Michael Graetz of Columbia Law School and David Henderson of the Naval Postgraduate School/Hoover Institute—*The Wall Street Journal* (2018), February 28, "Should the U.S. Adopt a Value-Added Tax?"

countries despite the presence of left-wing parties, powerful labor movements as well as strong anti-VAT conservative policy voices (economists educated in the USA or the "Chicago Boys"), plus USA and IMF hegemony since the 1970s, merits attention. Moreover, VAT increases consumer prices, and inflation, including episodes of hyperinflation, is a regional economic curse. Brazil's military dictatorship (1964–1985) prioritized rapid industrialization with a significant role for the public sector, or *developmentalism* (see Sikkink 1991), and it drew inspiration from European economic reconstruction in the 1950s and 1960s. Not lost on its neighbors, Brazil's VAT adoption coincided with Brazil's Economic Miracle (1968–1974) that made it the fastest industrializing economy in the world; psychologically impactful in a region desperate to reduce its dependency on primary commodity exports, Brazilian industrial exports surpassed coffee exports by the end of this period. Keen and Lockwood (2010) maintain that VAT diffuses in regional bursts tied to regional competition and early successes, and this seems to have occurred in South America.[9] Brazil's military regime's economic successes soon became a model for what Latin American observers refer to as bureaucratic-authoritarian regimes, and Brazil had a strong influence on military regimes in Argentina (1966–1973, 1976–1982) and Chile (1973–1990) (Malloy 1976; O'Donnell 1973; Collier 1979; Dávila 2013).

Argentina and Chile adopted their VATs in 1975, a chaotic time in the region as Argentina, Brazil and Chile as oil importers struggled after the 1973 OPEC oil crisis; however, national circumstances behind VAT decisions differed. On the heels of Brazil, Argentina's military government in 1968 sent a delegation to Europe with stops in France, Netherlands, Germany and Denmark to assess possible VAT adoption (World Bank 1987). The delegation's mixed report cast doubt on VAT's appropriateness in Argentina, and adoption was scrapped. Under elected civilian rule in December 1973, the iconic Juan Peron, back from exile in Spain and well-versed in the European VAT experience, designed and passed Argentina's VAT law—VAT collection began on January 1, 1975 (after Peron's death). VAT replaced a host of retail sales taxes that were prone to evasion; yet, income and corporate taxes remained the same. Peron headed a labor-based party, indeed, South America's most

[9]Other South American countries followed Brazil as well—Ecuador (1970), Bolivia (1973) and Peru (1973).

pro-labor party to reach national power, and he envisioned a progressive VAT. Exemptions for popular consumer items such as food and medicine and domestically produced goods would shift the tax burden more to urban middle-class and upper-class consumers and foreign corporations. In turn, obligatory VAT revenue sharing (following the Brazilian model) would redistribute VAT revenue from the wealthy capital of Buenos Aires to Peronist-dominated, and poorer, provincial governments.

In contrast, Chile under the conservative and strongly anti-labor Pinochet military dictatorship (1973–1990) adopted VAT as an opportunity to reduce income and corporate taxes in addition to advancing its general political goal of reversing Allende-era (1970–1973) societal reliance on the state. IMF public revenue reforms imposed across the region in the 1980s and 1990s diffused the Pinochet approach to VAT.[10] Allende was the only strict Marxist to win a free, democratic presidential election during the Cold War. The Pinochet dictatorship's perspective on VAT reversed the European logic: the popular sectors, it reasoned, would demand fewer public goods when they had to pay the bill by an inherently regressive form of taxation.

VAT performance initially varied. VAT quickly became a significant component of total taxation in Brazil and Chile, while prior to 1990, it did not in Argentina (World Bank 1990). As a percentage of total public revenue, in Argentina, traditional retail sales taxes were 19.3% in 1966, while the VAT was 19.0% in 1978 and 18.9% in 1985 (World Bank 1987: Table 2); by comparison, in Chile, VAT was 28.7% in 1979 and 31.4% in 1986 (Boylan 1996: Table 4), and in Brazil VAT hit 25.7% as early as 1975. Institutional considerations and regime instability contributed to this early variation (Melo 2007; Spiller and Tommasi 2007) more than cross-national variation in VAT rates, exemptions and enforcement (World Bank 1990; Cetrángolo and Gómez Sabaini 2010; Bergman 2003; Sánchez 2011). Stable Brazilian and Chilean military dictatorships designed, enacted and prioritized national VATs.

[10]Latin America adopted the neoliberal tax model. As a region between 1985 and 2015, tax rates plummeted for personal income tax (49.5–27.4%), corporate income tax (43.9–26.8%), and average tariff (49–4.3%), while the rate climbed for VAT (10.6–15.2%). Over the same period, regional tax-to-GDP marginally climbed and remains well below the OECD average (ECLAC 2016). The neoliberal tax model neither curtails regional economic crises nor promotes economic development as the region is more "commodity dependent" than ever while de-industrialization is a regional norm.

In Argentina, however, VAT was tethered to Peron and Peronism, the military's enemy during the Dirty War (1976–1982) and the opposition Radical party's rival during its time in power (1983–1989) (Spiller and Tommasi 2007).[11] Also, it should be emphasized that Brazil's initial experience with VAT coincided with a sustained economic boom so the "new tax" entered the public's consciousness amid its economic Golden Era—parallels exist between the European and Brazilian experiences. In contrast, Argentina's VAT adoption concurred with a period of sustain economic (and political) chaos, and its national VAT reboot in 1990–1991 occurred in a context of hyperinflation.

Argentina collects VAT at the federal level, and by law, a set percentage is shared with 23 provincial governments and the city of Buenos Aires (accorded provincial status) with the remaining revenue kept by the federal government. Income taxes have a similar arrangement. In contrast, excise trade taxes on agricultural exports are not shared with the provinces.[12] VAT collection in Brazil differs. Under Brazil's 1965 VAT law and revised 1988 VAT law, the 26 state governments (and the federal district is accorded state status) collect VAT and share revenue with municipalities at a rate of 25% under the 1988 law (Longo 1994). No VAT revenue goes to the federal government in Brazil. Argentina's subnational governments are incentivized to curb VAT revenue from their territory since federally collected and redistributed VAT revenue is guaranteed (i.e., let other provinces pay, especially wealthy Buenos Aires!), while Brazil's states must collect VAT or their own budgets suffer. Given these incentives, the outcome of higher evasion in Argentina and lower evasion in Brazil is to be expected. For example, in 1980, Argentina's military government, desperate to raise more tax revenue in the midst

[11] Political considerations are hard to dismiss in Argentina. Historical and other accounts stress the military government (1976–1982) and the Radical government (1983–1989) sought desperately to tame inflation and failed. More tax revenue to avoid printing pesos was constantly discussed, and the obvious policy choice should have been to replicate Chilean and Brazilian VAT policy. The first Peronist government post-Peron (i.e., the Menem government from 1989 to 1999) inheriting hyperinflation quickly ramped up VAT revenue (raised rate and broadened base to include food and services), and inflation dropped to its lowest rate in modern history.

[12] In a repeat of the 1980s, with the Radical party back in power and with the economy tanking in 2000 and 2001, President de la Rua reintroduced trade taxes on the agro-export sector rather than up the VAT rate or eliminate popular consumer exemptions. Reluctance to share revenue with Peronist governors no doubt factored into this decision.

of an economic crisis, broadened the VAT base and registered VAT tax payers jumped from 434,189 in 1979 to 824,638 in 1980; however, VAT-to-GDP changed little—3.1% in 1979, a brief up tick, and then back to 3.1% in 1983 (World Bank 1987, 1993). Contrast Argentina with Brazil, where as early as 1970, amidst a booming economy, Brazil's VAT-to-GDP hit 11.3%, and even as VAT revenue fell along with the performance of the Brazilian economy at the start of the 1980s VAT-to-GDP still doubled (7.1% in 1980) the rate in Argentina.

Bird and Zolt (2015: 323) state, "They [tax policies] reflect a rough political equilibrium among the various interests that shape policies." With current VAT rate regimes, it is possible to make a case that this is true in part in Argentina, Brazil and Chile. Today, Chile's uniform rate (19%) and no significant exemptions (voted top five worldwide for ease of use) contrasts with the multiple-rates and numerous exemptions found in Argentina and Brazil. Chile's VAT evasion rate falls below the OECD average (and has been since the early 1980s), while in Argentina and Brazil, it is above. Political scientists and multilateral observers depict the Chilean state and public bureaucracy as more autonomous from interest groups and less exposed to corruption and non-compliance than the situation in Argentina and Brazil (Bird 1992; Melo 2007).[13] Following the Weberian tradition, autonomous bureaucracies are a telltale sign of state capacity and modernization. In turn, Brazilian industrial groups have long exerted more influence over trade policy than their counterparts in Chile and Argentina. Brazil's multi-rate VAT regime levies a higher rate on imported goods (ranging from 17 to 25%) than on domestically produced and consumed goods (12%). Lastly, Argentina's political development pits labor unions embedded in the Peronist party against the country's agro-export sector and its service-oriented private sector concentrated in the city of Buenos Aires. In Argentina, imports and most consumer items are taxed at a standard VAT rate of 21%. A lower rate of 10.5% is applied to medical and most food items

[13]Teera and Hudson's (2004, Table 1) study of average tax-to-GDP ratios from 1975 to 1998 finds Chile (20.9%) and Brazil (17.2%) far outperforming Argentina (9.9%). Melo (2007) studies average tax-to-GDP from 1961 to 2003 in 24 similar income countries and concurs listing Argentina dead last. Medina and Schneider (2017) calculate the size of a country's shadow economy as a percentage of its GDP between 1991 and 2015, and Chile (18.2%) ranks better than Argentina (24.1%) and Brazil (37.6%). The above point to stronger state regulation and enforcement of rules via public bureaucracies.

(same rate on imported and domestic food items), including meat. Yet, all private businesses pay an increased rate of 27% on all their utilities (telecom, water, electricity and gas), while households pay the lower 21% rate on utilities.

Today, all three countries depend heavily on VAT to finance their public sectors and service their accumulated (and rising) foreign debts. In Brazil and Chile, VAT dependence started in the 1970s as only social security taxes have surpassed VAT, but in Argentina, it waited until 1990 when the government, mired in hyperinflation and desperate for World Bank and IMF assistance, scrapped traditional export taxes on the agricultural sector and broadened the VAT base and raised the standard rate (as advised by the World Bank in 1989). Both food (largest item of household consumption) and virtually all services (largest sector of the economy) were added to the VAT system in 1990, causing the share of GDP covered by the VAT system to rise from 52.2% in 1989 to 80% in 1992 (World Bank 1993). After 1990, and continuing to the present, Argentine VAT dependence has matched Brazilian and Chilean, and there is no reason to foresee VAT dependence diminishing any time soon.

Given VAT dependency, the challenge of evasion is paramount. VAT evasion rates exhibit cross-national variation and the Levi axiom (i.e., taxation is linked to state capacity) is a good guide. A study of European evasion rates finds institutionally strong Demark (4.2%) contrasts sharply with institutionally weak Italy (34.5%) (Gebaur, Nam, and Parsche 2003). And again, among our three case studies, Chile records far less VAT evasion than Brazil and Argentina. At the regional level, Latin America's VAT-to-GDP and VAT evasion-to-GDP are estimated at 6.8 and 2.4%, respectively, while the corresponding figures for combined Personal/Corporate income taxes and evasion are 6.8 and 4.3% (ECLAC 2016). VAT supporters original claim appears to be true, namely, VAT is harder to evade than personal income and corporate tax. VAT benefits by the fact that business collect the tax on behalf of the government, whereas the government itself must collect personal and corporate taxes.[14]

[14]This resembles feudal fiscal arrangements in Europe. North and Thomas (1973: 69) discuss England's Edward I borrowing 392,000 pounds from an Italian bank for the conquest of Wales. "It was the custom of kings to farm out their revenues." The Crown put the Italian bank in charge of collecting trade customs at British ports from 1272 to 1294 to

Gains in future VAT collection must be secured if the necessary investments in human capital (education, health, etc.), infrastructure and less debt-dependent economic development are to take place. Tax reform often implies changes in rates and exemptions as well as policy initiatives in the area of enforcement and tax morale. With rates and exemptions, our three case studies really do not have much room to maneuver. By Latin American and European standards, the main VAT rates in Argentina (21%), Brazil (17%) and Chile (19%) rank as high to modestly high and each extends coverage to nearly all products and services. Broadening national VAT coverage occurred in the 1980s and 1990s. Regular bureaucratic restructuring takes place and is expected to do so in the future; yet, if the past is prologue, scant additional revenue will result. Tax morale refers to the idea that public opinion and popular expectations associated with paying taxes can matter to tax revenue totals. Is it socially acceptable to evade taxes? There is a literature on this subject (Torgler 2005; Alm and Martinez-Vazques 2007; Torgler and Schneider 2009) and rooted in Robert Putnam's social capital framework (Putnam 1993, 2001). But such analyses, we believe, do not offer an advisable action plan to policy-makers, and public perceptions of tax are directly linked to the public's volatile views of economic conditions and general government performance.

To understand VAT evasion and how to reduce it, a place to start is to remember that VAT is a system and rarely a one-off transaction. Income taxes are due at a certain date (April 15 in the USA) and traditional sales taxes involve a retailor and a consumer at a moment in time. VAT begins at the start of the production process, continues at intermediary stages of production, and ends at final consumption, and the goal or advantage from a taxation perspective is that a VAT system creates a paper trail from start to finish. Take a simple example. A leather wholesaler sells leather to a cobbler, and in this transaction, the cobbler pays $100 for her leather. Our cobbler uses the leather to cobble a fancy handbag, she sells for $500 the handbag to a boutique clothing store in the capital city. Our cobbler submits to the tax authorities her $100 receipt for leather in order to get her VAT rebate.

repay the loan. Why? The Crown's capacity to collect tax was simply too weak or underdeveloped. Less evasion occurred with banks acting as the tax collector, and the Crown could avoid being the face of unpopular tax handovers.

A paper trail is the key feature of a national VAT system. In theory, the system creates a tangible financial incentive in the form of VAT rebates for actors to comply. If a business wants a tax refund, a receipt must be produced. However, the incentive to comply is uneven from start to finish. Our leather dealer and cobbler stand to gain financially and thus they often do comply with VAT rules. Also, government auditors are in a better position to investigate these intermediate transactions. Our boutique store retailer faces a different set of incentives. A store and the final customer can agree on a lower cash price outside of the VAT system and both will benefit—customer pays a lower price while the boutique pockets the cash and reports lower corporate income (i.e., lower corporate taxable income). No VAT rebate is coming and it is far more difficult for government auditors to enforce the law on such activities. Both retailers and consumers understand the norms and expectations around VAT and final consumption. "Hey, let's make a deal." It is final consumption that the shadow economy's impact on VAT is strongest, and it is here that policy-makers must focus their limited resources in order to secure needed VAT revenue in the future.

Financial Inclusion—Brief History and Ideologies

Financial inclusion is a policy framework for socioeconomic development that focuses on getting more people to use and have access to formal banking services. Since at least the 1970s, economic development specialists argued that financial inclusion should be targeted to "the poor or bottom of the pyramid" and mostly using microcredit loans. In this section, we outline the history of financial inclusion in the form of microcredit and how it has not succeeded in the way its proponents proclaimed. Then we present a new perspective on financial inclusion that targets middle-income families and how this approach has led to a variety of positive effects in Argentina, Brazil and Chile.

Financial inclusion typically implies a range of initiatives to deliver formal financial services such as banking (microcredit and microsavings), insurance, electronic money transfer, and electronic bill payments to excluded and underserved, mostly poor, populations at the bottom of the pyramid. "Approximately 2 billion adults, just below half of the world's adult population, are financially excluded" (Queralt et al. 2017: 2000). For advocates, by breaking the credit constraint that traps people in poverty, financial inclusion can be pivotal to alleviate poverty and spur sustainable market-based economic development (Hulme and Mosley 1996; Beck and Ogden 2007; GPFI 2011, 2016). For poorer households, investment either in human capital or in entrepreneurship requires access to credit. While financial inclusion discussions surfaced in the late 1970s, originally as microcredit programs and later as microfinance initiatives, current discussions are closely tied to twenty-first-century technologies such as smartphones and e-banking (see Realini and Mehta 2015) as well as financial globalization.

The United Nations (UN) declared 2005 as the International Year of Microcredit and in 2006, Muhammad Yunus won a Nobel Prize for his pioneering microcredit work in Bangladesh. Motivated by a global financial crisis in 2008 and 2009, the Group of 20 (G20) partnered with the multilateral development community to elevate financial inclusion to the top of the north–south poverty alleviation and economic development agenda (Soederberg 2013).[15] Speculative neoliberal financial instruments and actors torpedoed the global economy and threw millions into poverty in 2008 and 2009; nonetheless, the same cast of characters stood ready to alleviate future poverty! Soon, a consensus materialized as President Obama, Jeffrey Sachs, Muhammad Yunus, and Bono, among others, joined the G20, UN, IMF, World Bank, Inter-American Development Bank, Asian Development Bank, The Bill and Melinda Gates Foundation, The Clinton Foundation, The Grameen Foundation (global version of the Grameen Bank), Kiva and MicroPlace (global microlenders), American Enterprise Institute, CATO and Wall Street banks to proclaim that the poor, especially poor women, stood to benefit first and foremost from financial inclusion. Few cynics questioned this broad consensus.

Quickly, the G20 crafted the Global Partnership for Financial Inclusion (GPFI), a multilateral coordinating body (IMF, World Bank, UN, etc.) that produced in October 2011 its first white paper

[15] Microfinance, both its initial appearance and more recent multilateral promotion, is rooted in incoherent reactions to global financial crises. Microcredit first appeared in the developing world during the Debt Crisis of the late 1970s and 1980s. IMF structural adjustment eliminated state-run credit institutions, meaning microcredit emerged as traditional public credit programs for peasants and urban microenterprises collapsed. Meanwhile, the G20's embrace of microfinance occurred as public support in rich countries for traditional aid programs collapsed after the 2008–2009 global financial crisis. Microfinance, like microcredit, proved an unsuccessful substitute both for traditional public credit institutions and for traditional aid for the developed world.

titled *Standard-Setting and Financial Inclusion for the Poor—Toward Proportionate Standards and Guidance.*[16] Largely technical and attentive to financial system operations, nonetheless, optimism regarding future poverty alleviation infused the document. In March 2016, the GPFI produced a second white paper titled *Global Standard-Setting Bodies and Financial Inclusion—The Evolving Landscape*. "Evolving" hints at a noticeable shift among multilateral actors, as earlier unbridled optimism slowly got replaced, first, by soberer recognition of the potential dangers unregulated financial inclusion efforts pose to the fragile financial systems of developing countries and, second, by the small anticipated benefits in terms of poverty alleviation under best-case assumptions tied to financial inclusion. The World Bank's (see Cull and Morduch 2017) major report on the topic, titled "Microfinance and Economic Development" all but dismisses financial inclusion's potential to alleviate poverty. The UN tried to get in front of shifting sentiments by declaring 2012 as the Year of the Cooperative—collectively owned and less profitable than standard MFIs, such institutions exist across the developing world, and predate the microfinance movement. Microfinance always exhibits an urban bias due to cost considerations; yet, 70% of the world's poor are rural (Bastiaensen et al. 2013), and in Latin America, 50% of people at or below an annual GDP per capita of $2000 are agricultural workers (World Bank 2014: Fig. 1.1). Cautionary tales of financial inclusion-inspired programs keep surfacing, prompting critics to substitute the term micro*debt* for micro*credit,* and orthodox advocates to perform a sleight of hand by dropping the term microcredit in favor of the more neutral microfinance.[17]

[16]G20 interest kick-started other multilateral actors. See the Basel Committee for Banking Supervision's (2010) *Microfinance Activities and the Core Principles for Effective Banking Supervision* (Basel, Switzerland: Bank for International Settlements) and the World Bank's Consultative Group to Assist the Poor's (2012) *A Guide to Regulation and Supervision of Microfinance, Consensus Guidelines* (Washington, DC: World Bank).

[17]Discourse matters and reveals. Orthodox economists and multilateral agencies refer to government borrowing of money as debt—i.e., public sector debt and foreign debt—yet, individuals borrowing of money is credit. "Reckless government debt" is castigated; yet, individual "microcredit" is lauded. The Indian government can raise taxes and cut spending to repay loans (even reckless loans). Poor Indian households, with few entrepreneurial skills, with scant financial literacy, and with precarious socioeconomic circumstances, face hunger or worse to repay loans. Sleight of hand with terms is commonplace, most recently, when did "tax reform" replace "tax cuts" in popular discourse, and whose interests did it serve?

Jason Hickel's op-ed in *The Guardian* (2015, June 10) captures shifting views, "What's so fascinating about the microfinance craze is that it persists in the face of one unfortunate fact: microfinance doesn't work." Almost no evidence confirms the central and original claim of microfinance, namely, that *financial inclusion alleviates poverty*, and a growing body of evidence points in the opposite direction as borrowed sums at high interest rates must be repaid. Belatedly, the World Bank (see Cull and Morduch 2017: 3) agrees:

> Researchers...have so far failed to find sustained evidence that access to microfinance has *writ large* done much to reduce poverty, improve living conditions, and fuel micro-businesses. Nearly all rigorous quantitative studies, beginning well before the use of randomized controlled trials, fail to fully support microfinance as a tool that can powerfully and single-handedly reduce poverty.

Poor people, Hickel stresses and echoes others (see Dichter et al. 2007; Sinclair 2012; Roodman 2012), consume rather than invest microloans, greater than 90% of total microloans in countries as dissimilar as South Africa and Nicaragua (Weber 2004; Sinclair 2012). In 2012, Mexico's largest MFI (Compartamos) had 2.3 million borrowers and Angelucci et al. (2015: 155) found that around half were not microentrepreneurs. The World Bank (Cull and Morduch 2017: 4) acknowledges, "From customers' viewpoints, microfinance is already seen as providing basic household finance—even though in public documents lenders may describe microfinance as a tool strictly for entrepreneurial finance." In short, while MFIs peddle an entrepreneurial myth, an alternative reality exists on the ground. No European or US MFI, multilateral agency, US president or Hollywood actor markets microfinance with glossy photos of poor people purchasing TVs. TV purchases at usurious interest rates from for-profit microlenders based in the USA and Europe became far too common in India, Mexico, Nicaragua and Nigeria.

In our three case studies (Argentina, Brazil and Chile), the poor's consumption of durable goods contrasts with the ubiquitous consumption options enjoyed by middle class and above households of durables (TVs, washing machines, refrigerators, etc.) via no-interest, monthly quota payment schemes—examples include Rapipago and Pagofácil in Argentina and Chile. Microcredit fiascos in Nicaragua, Mexico, India and Indonesia coupled with allegations against the Grameen Bank in Bangladesh in 2011 altered perceptions of financial inclusion. As Bastiaensen et al (2013: 861) summarize, "The dominant verdict on microcredit has undergone a damning transformation, from 'magic bullet for poverty reduction' to 'cause of suicide'." Critical books by Hugh Sinclair (2012) and David Roodman (2012), both experienced microfinance practitioners, left many questioning the entire microcredit enterprise which stood as the main policy area to emerge under the more expansive financial inclusion multilateral push. Microsavings and microinsurance sectors, for example, pale in comparison to the giant microcredit sector that spans across the developing world.

Financial inclusion's recent troubles spread beyond microcredit. Kenya's touted M-Pesa cash transfer or mobile money scheme is, along with the Grameen Bank, lauded by financial inclusion advocates. Yet, the same program in 2016 collapsed in South Africa. M-Pesa in Kenya permits domestic cash transfers via smartphones and eliminates reliance on local money handlers. Kenyan villages with M-Pesa infrastructure, one study shows, registered lower (slightly) poverty than villages without the program over a period of six years (Suri and Jack 2016). Postmortem analysis of M-Pesa's collapse in South Africa, however, points to Kenya's concentrated telecom sector (one main carrier) versus South Africa's more developed and competitive telecom sector. Market concentration permits the economy of scale necessary for M-Pesa in Kenya to charge an attractive price and remain financially viable as a for-profit enterprise. Arabéhéty (2016) contends that South Africa resembles most Latin American and Caribbean markets, explaining why M-Pesa-type schemes perform poorly in the region. Returning to the second GPFI white paper in 2016, direct reference to the poor disappeared from the title and its executive summary, after two glossy photos of poor-looking women hard at work, scarcely mentions poverty alleviation.[18]

[18] Reality on the ground, especially in Latin America, caught up with multilateral actors by 2016. Microloan recipients too often used loans for consumption leaving poor households in debt. Governments in countries such as Nicaragua, Guatemala, Peru, Bolivia, Ecuador and Mexico faced protests from micro-borrowers (dramatically in Nicaragua) and caved, creating moral hazard. Added regulation of the sector to prevent reckless consumption (i.e., TV purchases via credit with an interest rate over 70%) is the obvious solution; yet, it contradicts the neoliberal model espoused by multilateral, local and Wall Street lenders.

Why financial inclusion might spur economic development and poverty alleviation is sensible *prima facie*: poor households benefit when family members in the cities can transfer cash cheaper and quicker to family members in rural areas (i.e., M-Pesa in Kenya), or when small microcredit loans permit poor households to purchase a cow to sell milk, hens to sell eggs or a cellphone to sell access to information (i.e., Grameen-style activities). Campbell (2010: 1089) argues, "Credit in the form of microfinance can elevate communities beyond subsistence agriculture or aid-reliance, nudging local economies toward the ultimate goal of healthy entrepreneurship and economic self-sufficiency and thus to having the financial wherewithal to access the same transformative technologies that have supported well-being in developed countries." Yet, microenterprise mythology, as its proponents (World Bank, IMF, IDB, etc.) acknowledge, has amounted to ideological wishful thinking. Connecting microcredit to the challenge of VAT collection, microbusinesses of the type referenced above operate inevitably in the shadow economy and in urban areas, they are apt to undermine formal businesses (see Sinclair 2012; Roodman 2012). A study that found microcredit did not lower poverty in India surmised, "[O]ne reason may be that the average business run by this target group is tiny (almost none of them have an employee), is not particularly profitable, and is difficult to expand even in a high-growth context, given the skill sets of the entrepreneurs and their life situations" (Banerjee et al. 2015: 51–52).

Bédécarrats et al. (2012: 154) analyze microfinance under leftist governments in Bolivia, Nicaragua and Ecuador, and note, "At the center is the debate on interest rates, described as exorbitant by movements whose social ethos does not sit well with poor people paying more than the rich. Microfinance providers are also criticized for their intransigent collection practices when it comes to dealing with recovering loans from poor clients prone to repayment difficulties." Some point out that traditional banks often offer large private firms bailouts and other favorable accommodations while microlenders force the poor to sell their tin roofs to meet the monthly or weekly payment. Whether microcredit charges a lower rate than loan sharks is contested by some (Sinclair 2012). Yunus himself sounded the alarm over Mexico's Banco Compartamos, an MFI with over 2.3 million micro-clients (by 2012) that charged interest rates in excess of 100%. Overall, Mexico's microcredit sector, according to Chuck Waterfield, CEO of the NGO Microfinance Transparency, saw interest rates average between 95 and 154% between 2004 and 2011.

Compartamos is something of a lightning rod. Proponents such as Matthew Gamser, Head, SME Finance Forum, argue that it is a financially viable for-profit model that extends credit to SMEs and by the fact that it continues to grow is a success. Critics highlight the high interest rates it charges, harsh collection norms and lavish corporate salaries (*The Economist* 2008, May 15; Sinclair and Matthew 2013; Angelucci et al. 2015). Does Latin America's largest for-profit MFI lower poverty? Nearly half the Mexican population lives below the poverty line, a higher percentage than in the 1970s despite slowing population growth in recent decades. And if Mexico's 2000-mile border with the USA did not permit large-scale outward migration from rural areas, the figure would be higher. Spectacular Compartamos growth coincides with no real improvement in poverty. Mexican poverty stood at 44.4% in 2008, 46.2% in 2014 and 43.6% in 2016, and the Mexican Social Development Ministry links the slight improvement to expansion in recent years of a conditional cash transfer (CCT) program rather than microcredit activities. Angelucci et al. (2015) study Compartamos lending and its impact on poverty in 238 geographic clusters in the state of Sonora, Mexico. The authors organized their study with Compartamos as the MFI entered Sonora and the results show no positive relationship on lowering poverty.

Financial inclusion in the form of microcredit has resulted in usurious interest rates and little (or no) effects on poverty alleviation. In many cases, microcredit makes poor families poorer by saddling them with debt. We do not advocate a complete reversal on microcredit. Under certain circumstances, it could be helpful and necessary. We do believe, however, that financial inclusion should be broadened and thought of in a different way—targeting more middle-income people rather than the poor. We also rely on a significant body of literature that finds a redistribution model (e.g., giving money directly to the poor in the form of CCT) has resulted in significant poverty alleviation—far greater than microcredit.

Financial Inclusion: The Middle of the Pyramid

Leading up to the 2008–2009 global financial crisis, the terms financial inclusion and microcredit were often used interchangeably. Microcredit, promoted by a Nobel Prize winner, celebrities and globally recognized NGOs since the late 1970s, promoted the neoliberal hope of the poor developing themselves and solving poverty themselves. As shown above, this approach has not worked. We argue that financial inclusion can be utilized to benefit a rival development model, one in which gains in economic development and poverty alleviation rest more on what development theorists, especially those in South America, refer to as developmentalism, where the state regulates, plans and strategizes how national resources are to be allocated in a market environment.

This chapter (and book) maintains that greater financial inclusion among middle-income people can help ameliorate the problem of low taxation by getting more people to use credit cards and debit cards to buy goods and services, thus shifting more consumption into formal markets and away from informal markets. In South America, from 2002 to 2014, Argentina's shadow economy as a percentage of GDP went from 26.9% down to 22% (an 18.2% relative reduction), Brazil's went from 38.5% down to 33% (a 14.3% reduction) and Chile's went from 18.3% down to 12.7% (a 30.6% reduction). In Europe too, more cards and less cash have been shown to reduce VAT evasion and shadow economies. Schneider and Kearney (2013) show that inside Europe, the size of the shadow economy correlates with the number of electronic transactions per person per year—i.e., more electronic transactions, smaller shadow economies. VAT's significance across Europe—EU rules require members to have a national VAT— means reducing evasion is a priority. Sung et al. (2017) find that electronic transactions reduce the shadow economy in South Korea; it is the rich country (along with Denmark) that pushes the cashless agenda furthest. This is a radical new notion in the context of the current financial inclusion debate and literature. More tax revenue and the commitment of a developmentalist state that redistributes wealth and prioritizes lower poverty and inequality via public programs—such as conditional cash transfers (CCTs), popular or informal sector pensions, public works, and expanded access to education and health services—are, in our view, the most promising and prudent path to economic development and lower poverty. In short, financial inclusion conceived as the poor embracing entrepreneurship to solve their own problems, or what neoliberals deem as financial inclusion at the bottom of the pyramid, strike us as misguided and doomed to fail.

Domestic institutional weaknesses and political realities surrounding tax collection together with the increasing global mobility of capital mean taxing consumption will, as it has for decades, surpass alternative types of taxation (income, profits and property). Historical experience teaches us that taxing income and property is difficult and inefficient in South America. Orthodox research (largely produced by Americans) decries the regressive quality of consumption taxes, given that the poor spend more and save less of their income compared to wealthier households. But this conclusion falls victim to the "snap shot" fallacy—that is, drawing conclusions from one-off moments in time. Swedes, Dutch and Germans enjoy lower levels of poverty and inequality compared to the United States, yet collect high consumption taxes. Beer, gas and clothes are all more expensive in Europe due to consumption taxes. However, if consumption taxes fund generous social welfare states that disproportionately benefit the people at the bottom of the pyramid, as they do in continental Europe, then the potential cost–benefit analysis of consumption taxes to the poor shifts.

Microcredit as a poverty reduction policy has not held up to empirical scrutiny. There is a method of poverty alleviation that has proven effective in Latin America: CCTs. The basic CCT model combines monthly cash handouts to poor families who keep children in school and maintain regular health check-ups. Data that follow are taken from the CEPAL report *Conditional cash transfer programmes in Latin America and the Caribbean* (Cecchini and Atuesta 2017). Brazil in three cities piloted the first CCT in 1995 and Mexico created the first national CCT, called Progresa, in 1997 (on Progresa see Mitchell 2001; Levy 2006). By 2015, national CCTs operated in thirty Latin American countries and one-fifth of the region's population, or 132 million people and 30 million households, received benefits. Among our three case studies, Chile (2002) launched a national CCT first followed by Brazil (2003) and Argentina (2005). By 2015, the percentage of the total population in CCTs stretched to a remarkable 27.9% in Brazil and 24% in Argentina, yet only 1.8% in Chile (lowest in Latin America). On the issue of cash transferred, by 2015, the per-person annual total in Argentina reached US$371, Brazil reached US$146 and Chile reached US$250. Thus, a family of four received US$1484 in Argentina, US$584 in Brazil and US$1000 in Chile. According to the World Bank, on a per-capita basis, extreme poverty amounts to $1.25 per day or $456 annually; thus, the CCT revenue transferred is not insignificant and it did not exist in our three case studies before 2002.

The World Bank (2013) report *The Rise of the Latin American Middle Class* attributes demand-generating CCTs with pulling 70 million people above the poverty line after 2002, and lifted 50 million people into the middle class between 2003 and 2009. Measured as the share of population living on less than US$3.20 per day (World Bank/statista data) between 2002 and 2014, our case studies experienced a dramatic improvement: Argentina from 26.3 to 4.5%, Brazil from 25.3 to 7.9%, and Chile from 11.65 and 2.85%. Overall income inequality measured by the Gini coefficient registered similar gains. From 2002 to 2014, Argentina's Gini coefficient decreased from 48.6 to 38.5 (a 20.8% reduction); Brazil from 56.3 to 50.1 (an 11% decline); and Chile from 40.7 to 39 (a 4.2% reduction). The World Bank contends that current government spending is unsustainable and necessitates a regional u turn back to the supply-side policies of the 1990s. We disagree and maintain that mobilizing more tax revenue is the better strategy. Direct CCT payments to poor people rely on a demand-side effect on poverty where poor people are simply trying to survive—which is why most microcredit loans went toward consumption rather than investment. People struggle to feed and clothe their children and themselves, so cash payments soften the extreme poverty that exists in many parts of the region. One multilateral study theorizes that redistribution of VAT revenue through CCTs ensures that, contrary to conventional thinking, VAT can be progressive (see Barreix et al. 2011).[19] We agree.

Our research findings show that getting more middle-income people into the banking system in Argentina, Brazil and Chile has resulted in significant increases in electronic payments, which is correlated with rising VAT revenue since the early 2000s. States then redistributed a portion of this money in the form of direct money transfers (e.g., CCTs), which coincided with significant decreases in inequality and poverty

[19]Barreix et al. (2011: 8) are correct that "[U]ltimately the progressive or regressive nature of a country's fiscal policy is an empirical matter that reflects a society's political consensus." Steinmo (1993) in *Taxation and Democracy*, his influential book on taxation in the USA and Europe, reaches the same conclusion. Simply put, VAT is progressive when governments transfer sufficient VAT revenue back to the lower classes, and in Latin America, CCTs are the obvious means to do this, given their track record of lowering poverty and boosting consumption at the bottom of the pyramid. Progressive VATs exist in Europe, Canada, Australia and elsewhere (see Goni et al. 2008). Consider the top three countries in the 2018 United Nations Human Development Index (broad measure of national welfare): Norway with a national VAT of 25%, Switzerland with a national VAT of 7.7%, and Australia with a national VAT of 10%. Also see ECLAC/Oxfam, *Time to Tax for Inclusive Growth* (2016) and Keen (2012).

levels. While current debates over financial inclusion might be multifaceted, our contribution is restricted to the role financial inclusion plays on VAT collection in South America. In particular, thinking about financial inclusion in South America as a middle-of-the-pyramid strategy to get more people using formal banking services that increases formal consumption will improve VAT efficiency. Perhaps equally important, it also stabilizes the tax base so the government is able to plan and spend knowing what their budgets will be and thus not rely on borrowing when revenues fall short.

Conclusion

More and stable tax revenue is the challenge all developing countries face. Bahl and Bird (2008: Table 1) emphasize a persistent gap between industrialized and developing countries in terms of tax revenue-to-GDP percentage—1970s (indust 30.1%/dev 16.2%), 1980s (indust 33.7%/dev 17.3%), 1990s (indust 35.5%/dev 17%) and 2000s (indust 33.4%/dev 17%). More tax revenue, following Levi, is a requisite of a modern state; it permits investment in its people, institutions and infrastructure in ways that support economic and political modernization. Less revenue means developing countries neither secure property rights nor invest in basic political institutions (courts, police, tax collectors, etc.), human capital or infrastructure. Perhaps equally discomfiting is that when South American countries are not able to collect adequate tax revenue, it makes them vulnerable to financial crisis. Reductions in government revenue means many governments deficit spend hoping that the shortfall is temporary. If not, then the macroeconomy can become unstable. Spillover effects can quickly result in a loss of confidence in the government and economy both domestically and globally. The repercussions include currency devaluation, IMF loans and high interest rates to attract foreign investors. While many people believe that improving tax collections in South America is all but impossible, we find that South American's heavy reliance on VAT means that recent increases in financial inclusion (e.g., bank accounts, credit cards and debit cards) are shifting increasing amounts of consumption from informal markets into formal markets, resulting in an elevated and more stable VAT revenue stream. Looking to the future, with large shadow economies still present in our three case studies, the potential for more VAT revenue exists and needs to be a priority of policy-makers.

References

Aaron, H., ed. 1981. *The Value-Added Tax: Lessons from Europe*. Washington, DC: The Brookings Institution.

Acemoglu, D., and J. A. Robinson. 2012. *Why Nations Fail: The Origins of Power, Prosperity, and Poverty*. New York: Crown Business.

Alm, J., and J. Martinez-Vazques. 2007. "Tax Morale and Tax Evasion in Latin America." Andrew Young School of Policy Studies, George State University, International Studies Program, Working Paper 07-04, March.

Angelucci, M., D. Karlan, and J. Zinman. 2015. "Microcredit Impacts: Evidence from a Randomized Microcredit Program Placement Experiment by Compartamos Banco." *American Economic Journal: Applied Economics* 7 (1) (January): 151–182.

Arabéhéty, P. G. 2016. "The Replication Limits of M-Pesa in Latin America." *CGAP Blog*, July 20. https://www.cgap.org/blog/replication-limits-m-pesa-latin-america.

Bahl, R. W., and R. M. Bird. 2008. "Tax Policy in Developing Countries: Looking Back and Forward." Institute for International Business Working Paper Series (IIB Paper No.13), May.

Banerjee, A., E. Duflo, R. Glennerster, and C. Kinnan. 2015. "The Miracle of Microfinance? Evidence from a Randomized Evaluation." *American Economic Journal: Applied Economics* 7 (1): 22–53.

Barreix, A., M. Bés, and J. Roca. 2011. Solving the Impossible Trinity of Consumption Taxes, Personalized VAT. ECLAC, United Nations, September.

Bastiaensen, J., P. Marchetti, R. Mendoza, and F. Pérez. 2013. After the Nicaraguan Non-Payment Crisis: Alternatives to Microfinance Narcissism. *Development and Change* 44 (4): 861–885.

Bates, R. 2001. *Prosperity and Violence*. New York: W.W. Norton.

Beck, S., and T. Ogden. 2007. "Beware of Bad Microcredit." *Harvard Business Review* 85 (9): 20–22.

Bédécarrats, F., J. Bastiaensen, and F. Doligez. 2012. "Co-optation, Cooperation or Competition? Microfinance and the New Left in Bolivia, Ecuador and Nicaragua." *Third World Quarterly* 33 (1): 143–160.

Bergman, M. 2003. "Tax Reforms and Tax Compliance: The Divergent Paths of Chile and Argentina." *Journal of Latin American Studies* 35 (3): 593–624.

Besley, T., and T. Persson. 2009. "The Origins of State Capacity: Property Rights, Taxation and Politics." *American Economic Review* 99 (4): 1218–1244. ISSN 0002-8282. https://doi.org/10.1257/aer.99.4.1218.

Besley, T., and T. Persson. 2013. "Taxation and Development." In *Handbook of Public Economics*, vol. 5, 51–110. https://doi.org/10.1016/B978-0-444-53759-1.00002-9.

Bird, R. M. 1992. "Tax Reform in Latin America: A Review of Some Recent Experiences." *Latin American Research Review* 27 (1): 7–36.

Bird, R. M., and P. P. Gendron. 2007. *The VAT in Developing and Transitional Countries*. Cambridge: Cambridge University Press.

Bird, R. M., and E. M. Zolt. 2015. "Fiscal Contracting in Latin America." *World Development* 67: 323–335.

Boylan, D. M. 1996. "Taxation and Transition: The Politics of the 1990 Chilean Tax Reform." *Latin American Research Review* 31 (1): 7–31.

Brautigam, D., O. H. Fjeldstad, and M. Moore. 2008. *Taxation and State-Building in Developing Countries: Capacity and Consent*. Cambridge: Cambridge University Press.

Campbell, G. 2010. "Microfinancing the Developing World: How Small Loans Empower Local Economies and Catalyse Neoliberalism's Endgame." *Third World Quarterly* 31 (7): 1081–1090.

Cecchini, S., and B. Atuesta. 2017. *Conditional Cash Transfer Programmes in Latin America and the Caribbean*. CEPAL. Social Policy Series. ISSN 1680-8983. United Nations.

Cetrángolo, O., and J. C. Gómez Sabaini. 2010. "Tax Policy in Argentina: Between Solvency and Emergency." *Taxation in Developing Countries: Six Case Studies and Policy Implications* 62–108.

Collier, D., ed. 1979. *The New Authoritarianism in Latin America*. Princeton: Princeton University Press.

Cull, R., and J. Morduch. 2017. Microfinance and Economic Development. Policy Research Working Paper; No. 8252. World Bank, Washington, DC. https://openknowledge.worldbank.org/handle/10986/28913. License: CC BY 3.0 IGO.

Dávila, J. 2013. *Dictatorship in South America*. London: Wiley-Blackwell.

de La Feria, R. 2009. *The EU VAT System and the Internal Market*, vol. 16. IBFD.

de Soto, H. 1989. *The Other Path: The Economic Answer to Terrorism*. New York: Harper & Row Publishers.

Dichter, T., and M. Harper, eds. 2007. *What's Wrong With Microfinance?* Eastbourne: Intermediate Technology Publications Ltd.

Dioda, L. 2012. "Structural Determinants of Tax Revenue in Latin America and the Caribbean, 1990–2009." ECLAC, December 2012. Regional Headquarters Mexico City, 2012-041.

Ebrill, L. P., M. Keen, J. P. Bodin, and V. P. Summers, eds. 2001. *The Modern VAT*. International Monetary Fund.

ECLAC. 2016. Economic Survey of Latin America and the Caribbean: The 2030 Agenda for Sustainable Development and the Challenges of Financing for Development, United Nations. ISBN: 978-92-1-057543-0.

ECLAC/Oxfam. 2016. *Time to Tax for Inclusive Growth*, March. Washington, DC.

Fuest, C., G. R. Zodrow, eds. 2013. *Critical Issues in Taxation and Development*. Cambridge: The MIT Press.

Gillis, M., ed. 1989. *Tax Reform in Developing Countries*. Durham: Duke University Press.

Goni, E., H. Lopez, and L. Serven. 2008. Fiscal Redistribution and Income Inequality in Latin America. World Bank Policy Research Working Paper No. 4487, World Bank, Washington, DC.

GPFI. 2011. *Standard-Setting and Financial Inclusion for the Poor—Toward Proportionate Standards and Guidance*. Washington, DC. October.

GPFI. 2016. *Global Standard-Setting Bodies and Financial Inclusion—The Evolving Landscape*. Washington, DC. March.

Huntington, S. P. 1968. *Political Order in Changing Societies*. New Haven: Yale University Press.

Kaldor, N. 1963. "Taxation for Economic Development." *Journal of Modern African Studies* 1: 7–12.

Keen, M. 2012. *Taxation and Development—Again*. IMF Working Paper, WP/12/220, Washington, DC.

Keen, M., and B. Lockwood. 2010. "The Value Added Tax: Its Causes and Consequences." *Journal of Development Economics* 92 (2): 138–151.

Levi, M. 1988. *Of Rule and Revenue*, vol. 13. University of California Press.

Levy, S. 2006. *Progress Against Poverty: Sustaining Mexico's Progresa-Oportunidades Program*. Brookings Institution Press.

Lipset, S. M. 1959. "Some Social Requisites of Democracy: Economic Development and Political Legitimacy." *The American Political Science Review* 53 (1) (March): 69–105.

Longo, C. A. 1994. "Federal Problems with VAT in Brazil." *Revista brasileira de economia* 48 (1): 85–106.

Lustig, N., and D. McLeod. 2009. *Are Latin America's New Left Regimes Reducing Inequality Faster?* Washington, DC: Woodrow Wilson Center for International Scholars, Latin American Program, Julio.

Mahon, J. E. 2004. "Causes of tax reform in Latin America, 1977–95." *Latin American Research Review* 3–30.

Malloy, J., ed. 1976. *Authoritarianism and Corporatism in Latin America*. University of Pittsburgh Press.

Medina, L., and F. G. Schneider. 2017. Shadow Economies Around the World: New Results for 158 Countries Over 1991–2015, April 10. CESifo Working Paper Series No. 6430. Available at SSRN: https://ssrn.com/abstract=2965972.

Melo, M. A. 2007. "Institutional Weakness and the Puzzle of Argentina's Low Taxation." *Latin American Politics and Society* 49 (4): 115–148.

Migdal, J. S. 1988. *Strong Societies and Weak States: State-Society Relations and State Capabilities in the Third World*. Princeton: Princeton University Press.

Mitchell, K. E. 2001. *State-Society Relations in Mexico: Clientelism, Neoliberal State Reform, and the Case of Conasupo*. London: Ashgate.

Mosley, P., and D. Hulme. 1996. *Finance Against Poverty*, vol. 1. London: Routledge.

North, D. 1990. *Institutions, Institutional Change and Economic Performance*. Cambridge: Cambridge University Press.

North, D., and R. P. Thomas. 1973. *The Rise of the Western World, A New Economic History*. Cambridge: Cambridge University Press.

O'Donnell, G. 1973. *Modernization and Bureaucratic-Authoritarianism*. Berkeley: University of California Press.

OECD. 2018. Revenue Statistics in Latin America and the Caribbean 2018. https://dx.doi.org/10.1787/rev_lat_car-2018-en-fr.

Putnam, R. D. 1993. *Making Democracy Work, Civic Traditions in Modern Italy*. Princeton: Princeton University Press.

Putnam, R. D. 2001. *Bowling Alone: The Collapse and Revival of American Community*. Simon and Schuster.

Queralt, J., J. Fu, and M. Romano. 2017. "Financial Inclusion and the 2030 Agenda for Sustainable Development: A Missed Opportunity." *Enterprise Development and Microfinance* 28 (3): 200–211.

Realini, C., and K. Mehta. 2015. *Financial Inclusion at the Bottom of the Pyramid*. Friesen Press.

Rogoff, K. S. 2017. *The Curse of Cash: How Large-Denomination Bills Aid Crime and Tax Evasion and Constrain Monetary Policy*. Princeton University Press.

Roodman, D. M. 2012. *Due Diligence: An Impertinent Inquiry Into Microfinance*. CGD Books.

Sánchez, O. 2011. *Mobilizing Resources in Latin America: The Political Economy of Tax Reform in Chile and Argentina*. Springer.

Schneider, F., and A. T. Kearney. 2013. "The Shadow Economy in Europe, 2013." *Johannes Kepler Universitat*. Linz.

Sikkink, K. 1991. *Ideas and Institutions, Developmentalism in Brazil and Argentina*. Ithaca: Cornell University Press.

Sinclair, H., and G. Matthew. 2013. "Crossfire: 'Should Financial Inclusion Be Part of the Next Set of MDGs?'." *Enterprise Development and Microfinance* 24 (4): 275–281.

Sinclair, H. 2012. *Confessions of a Microfinance Heretic: How Microlending Lost Its Way and Betrayed the Poor*. Berrett-Koehler Publishers.

Slemrod, J. 2011. "Does a VAT Promote Exports?" *Tax Analysts* 186.

Soederberg, S. 2013. "Universalising Financial Inclusion and the Securitisation of Development." *Third World Quarterly* 34 (4): 593–612.

Spiller, P. T., and M. Tommasi. 2007. *The Institutional Foundations of Public Policy in Argentina*. Cambridge: Cambridge University Press.

Steinmo, S. 1993. *Taxation & Democracy: Swedish, British, and American Approaches to Financing the Modern State*. New Haven: Yale University Press.

Sung, M. J., R. Awasthi, and H. C. Lee. 2017. *Can Tax Incentives for Electronic Payments Reduce the Shadow Economy?* World Bank Group. WPS7936, Washington, DC. January.

Suri, T., and W. Jack. 2016. "The Long-Run Poverty and Gender Impacts of Mobile Money." *Science* 354 (6317): 1288–1292.

Tanzi, V. 2007. *Argentina: An Economic Chronicle*. New York: Pinto Books.

Tanzi, V. 2013. *Tax Reform in Latin America: A Long Term Assessment*. CEQ Working Paper, No. 15.

The Economist. 2008. "Poor People, Rich Returns." May 15.

The Guardian. 2015. "The Microfinance Delusion: Who Really Wins?" June 10.

The Wall Street Journal. 2018. "Should the U.S. Adopt a Value-Added Tax?" February 28.

Teera, J. M., and J. Hudson. 2004. "Tax Performance: A Comparative Study." *Journal of International Development* 16 (6): 785–802.

Tilly, C. 1990. *Coercion, Capital, and European States, AD 990-1990*. Oxford. Blackwell.

Torgler, B. 2005. "Tax Morale in Latin America." *Public Choice* 122 (1–2): 133–157.

Torgler, B., and F. Schneider. 2009. "The Impact of Tax Morale and Institutional Quality on the Shadow Economy." *Journal of Economic Psychology* 30 (2): 228–245.

Weber, H. 2004. "The 'New Economy' and Social Risk: Banking on the Poor?" *Review of International Political Economy* 11 (2): 356–386.

World Bank. 1987. The Argentinean Experience With The Value-Added Tax. Discussion Paper No. DRD235, Washington, DC.

World Bank. 1990. Argentina, Tax Policy for Stabilization and Economic Recovery. Pub8067, Washington, DC.

Word Bank. 1993. Effects of Tax Reform on Argentina's Revenues. WPS 1192, Washington, DC.

World Bank. 2013. The Rise of the Latin American Middle Class. Washington, DC.

World Bank. 2014. Emerging Issues in Financial Development, Lessons from Latin America. Working Paper 83498, Washington, DC.

World Health Organization. 2017. Earmarking for Health, From Theory to Practice. WHO Health Financing Working Paper No. 5.

CHAPTER 2

Public Revenue, Financial Inclusion and Value-Added Tax in Argentina

Abstract Argentina's tax-to-GDP ratio ranked at the bottom of worldwide tables of middle-income countries prior to the 2000s. By 2015, Argentina transformed from a low-tax to a high-tax country matching Brazil for the highest tax-to-GDP ratio in the region. No tax expert anticipated this outcome—quite the opposite. A rise in Value-Added Tax (VAT) revenue occurred as overall tax revenue increased, and this trend continued after a period of economic growth ended. This chapter explains how the government engineered this result by way of financial inclusion measures that targeted middle-class Argentines and their inclusion into the formal banking system. As financial inclusion drew more people into the formal banking system, consumers began to use less cash and more credit and debit cards causing more consumption to occur in formal markets ("easily taxed") and less in informal markets ("less taxed").

Keywords Argentina · Value-added tax (VAT) · Informal market · Financial inclusion · Banks · Credit cards · Banking cards

Introduction

Argentina is South America's second largest economy behind Brazil, and its agricultural exports rank near the top of world tables (2017)—soybean oil (#1), soymeal for livestock (#1), soybeans and

K. Mitchell and R. H. Scott, III, *Pesos or Plastic?*,
https://doi.org/10.1007/978-3-030-14876-8_2

corn (#3), beef (#6), wheat (#7) and wine (#10). Argentine soymeal feeds 50% of UK and 33% of European Union livestock. Argentine agricultural exports rival the USA and Brazil, although its population is far smaller—44 million compared to 325 million (USA) and 209 million (Brazil). Despite its advantageous agricultural resources and small population, Argentina endures periodic economic crises on a grand scale—600% inflation in 1976, 672% inflation in 1985, 200% inflation in the month of July in 1989, 20,000% inflation in 1990, the world's largest sovereign default at the time in December 2001 (Greece later surpassed it), and the IMF's largest loan (US$57 billion) in September 2018—as well as more generalized and protracted economic decline. Argentina's allure, in part, is its experience of economic un-development. Around 1930, Argentina ranked among the world's wealthiest countries, its agro-export sector generated hard currency, its large British-funded rail network opened up new tracks of lands for harvest, and its propitious ratio of population to productive land kept wages higher than in Europe which attracted coveted waves of European immigrants.

Today, however, Argentina is now much poorer (60th wealthiest country based on GDP per capita in 2017) and decades of de-industrialization mean that the economy is more dependent than ever on commodity exports. Complicating matters, around 97% of Argentines reside in cities and agricultural commodity dependence serves to exasperate rural–urban tensions that have destabilized national politics and policy-making since independence in 1816 (Rock 1987; Calvert and Calvert 1989; Di Tella and Dornbusch 1989; Cortés Conde 2013).[1] Argentina's requisite first-step toward more sound and successful economic management and future development is to resolve its long-running public revenue problem. Low tax revenue, we maintain, while not the only cause of Argentina's economic troubles, did contribute

[1]Argentina in the twentieth century experienced six military coups (1930, 1943, 1955, 1962, 1966, and 1976); the last produced the military regime responsible for the Dirty War (1976–1983) and an estimated 30,000 Argentine deaths. Each coup had strong rural elite support and military regimes disproportionately targeted their violence toward urban political groups—labor unions, lawyers, university students and professors, and intellectuals—as well as implemented economic policies favorable to the agro-export sector. Also, Argentine coups are rooted in intra-military conflicts, these tended to pit the army, which heavily recruited from the interior, against the navy, which heavily recruited from the urban middle classes. Besides the Dirty War horrors, rapid urbanization and a dwindling rural population help to account for the lack of a military coup since 1983.

significantly to the country's twin evils over the past several decades, namely, a propensity to borrow unsustainable amounts in US dollars from abroad and to print too many pesos at home. Argentine tax collection is unusual.[2] More specifically, while Argentine tax revenue remained extremely low by regional and worldwide standards in the 1970s, 1980s and 1990s, the country reversed and sustained dramatically higher tax revenue levels thereafter, a shift that analysts neither anticipated nor explain convincingly.

How low is low? A study of 24 similar income countries between 1961 and 2003, a span that saw the country adopt almost every conceivable economic orientation from neoliberal to statist, finds Argentina *with the lowest tax-to-GDP ratio* or so-called tax ratio (Melo 2007: 115). A larger study of average tax ratios from 1975 to 1998 finds that, first, Argentina (9.9%) ranks well below other South American countries such as Brazil (17.2%), Venezuela (17.4%), Chile (20.9%) and Uruguay (24%), and, second, among all upper middle-income countries worldwide Argentina ranks only ahead of Bahrain (7.5%) (Teera and Hudson 2004, see Tables 1 and A4). At the end of 1980s, its tax system had essentially collapsed, a mere 30,000 of 30 million Argentines paid any income tax. Most accept that economic modernization and development rest on effective tax collection in order to pay for, at minimum, essential public goods such as infrastructure (ports, roads, railways, irrigation, and electricity), human capital investment (i.e., education and health), nascent industries, and property rights protections (North and Thomas 1973; Levi 1988; Migdal 1988; Steinmo 1993; Brautigam et al. 2008; Acemoglu and Robinson 2012). This view holds true in South America as analysts concur that the best-run economies in the region are the higher tax revenue countries of Chile and Uruguay. Had Argentina's tax ratio in the 1970s, 1980s and 1990s matched that of Chile and Uruguay, it could have averted many of its economic problems.

[2]The political science literature links high tax revenue in a country to the strength of left-center and labor-based political parties, urbanization and the strength and autonomy of the state (see Steinmo 1993; Brautigam et al. 2008). Europe's social democratic parties inspire this literature. By these assumptions, however, Argentina's tax revenue during the past several decades should have been high. The pro-labor Peronist Party has been the strongest political force since the 1940s, rapid urbanization started in the 1950s, and state capacity is demonstrated by the country's healthcare and education systems that were regional leaders in the twentieth century.

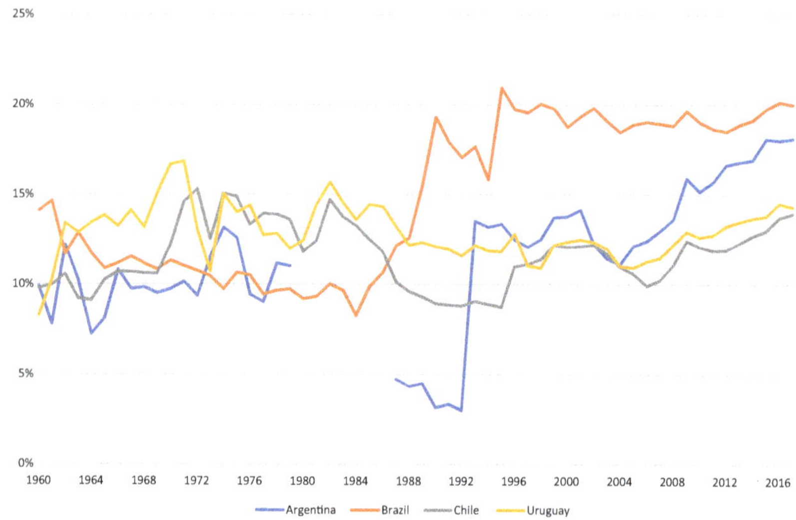

Fig. 2.1 Government spending-to-GDP for Argentina, Brazil, Chile and Uruguay, 1960–2017 (TheGlobalEconomy 2018)

Multilateral actors and international investors maintain that excessive Argentine government spending spurred its frequent economic crises. But this is inaccurate—and shifts attention from the issue of low tax revenue. As we see in Fig. 2.1, Argentine government spending as a percentage of GDP ("spending ratio") falls below Brazil, Chile and Uruguay during the 1970s and 1980s, and it only matches Chile and Uruguay (not Brazil) in the 1990s.[3] From 1986 to 1992, Argentina's spending ratio hovered below 5% (bottoming out at 2.98% in 1992) while that of its neighbors ranged from 10 to 15%. In short, an accurate picture finds

[3]Three annual snapshots at decade intervals show trends in government spending-to-GDP in the Southern Cone countries of South America: *1977* (Argentina 9.02%, Brazil 9.44%, Chile 13.94%, and Uruguay 12.74%), *1987* (Argentina 4.71%, Brazil 12.16%, Chile 10.12%, and Uruguay 13.22%) and *1997* (Argentina 12.06%, Brazil 19.54%, Chile 11.12%, and Uruguay 11.04%). Argentine government spending was lower than that of its neighbors, especially so in the 1980s, and this pattern only changed, oddly, after Argentina adopted radical neoliberal liberalization policies in the 1990s at which point, Argentina caught up with Chile and Uruguay, but remained well behind Brazil. Finally, counter to conventional wisdom, Argentine annual spending ratios in 2016 (18.03%) and 2017 (18.11%) under current neoliberal President Macri were *the two highest years since 1960*!

that the Argentine government spent less than its neighbors but it also collected significantly less tax revenue than its neighbors. Against this backdrop, Argentina's tax ratio from 2003 to 2015 *began* at a low rate, even by Argentine standards, in an environment of economic turmoil after the world's largest sovereign default in December 2001, and *ended* at the highest level in South America after thirteen years of heterodox economic policies and, critically, international financial market exile starting in 2002 that produced acute urgency around tax collection.

Has Argentina solved its tax problem? Potentially it has and its experience can provide lessons for other countries. This chapter explains *how* the turnaround came about (exile from global financial markets, value-added tax [VAT] gains, financial inclusion policies, consumer behavior shifts and currency controls), *why* the turnaround is significant (less poverty, less inequality, less informal sector economic activity, and less borrowing abroad in US dollars), and finally, *whether* the turnaround can be sustained given the structural realities of Argentina's commodity-dependent economy.

Argentina's recent tax ratio gains largely resulted from government measures that improved the performance of its main tax revenue stream—the VAT. In the sections that follow, these efforts are discussed in detail. But it is hard to find in the literature a convincing explanation for Argentina's recent VAT gains. Argentina's VAT as a percentage of total taxation resembles European countries, but how it operates differs; Argentina's small industrial base and exemptions for strategic, often region-specific domestic producers mean that VAT functions more as a tax on final consumption, notably on consumption of imported products, than on value-added associated with domestic production chains. VAT revenue tends to be pro-cyclical, rising and falling with economic growth and imports. However, and this is a key issue in this chapter, VAT revenue reached historic highs as a percentage of GDP ("VAT ratio") between 2003 and 2015 despite, starting in 2010, unchanged VAT rates, slow economic growth, stagnant household consumption, import controls and low commodity prices. In short, VAT revenue around 2010 should have dropped fast, but instead it stayed elevated. Why?

Our answer is unorthodox. Analysts concur that VAT climbed between 2002 and 2009 due in large part to a global commodity boom spurring economic recovery and growth, more household consumption and more imports. In the past, indeed, VAT and total tax revenue did plummet along with the macroeconomy, often pushing Argentina from economic instability to full-blown economic crisis—the tax ratio fell before crises in the 1970s, 1980s, 1990s and before the epic 2001–2002 collapse. IMF teams dispatched to Buenos Aires repeatedly implored Argentina to elevate its tax ratio—all without success.

In 2015, VAT revenue accounted for one-quarter of all tax revenue in Argentina, an all-time high. Financial inclusion policies advanced by the government after 2002 established the conditions to secure this outcome; notably, Argentina's banked population (i.e., "adults with a bank account") jumped from 41.6% in 2003 to 89.6% in 2016. Financial inclusion, a worldwide movement that started in the 1970s, focuses universally on the bottom of the pyramid (i.e., the poor) and extending to it microcredit and cashless money transfer technologies (see Chapter 1 above). However, drawing people into the formal banking system, the thrust of financial inclusion in Argentina, had an important consequence involving the *middle* of the pyramid—or, the middle and formal working classes—namely, by moving a sizeable percentage of their daily consumption from cash to card-based transactions. Rapid growth in electronic consumer transactions and other purchases (for example, small business purchases of intermediate goods) via credit cards and debit cards occurred after 2002. Our time-series regression tests later in the chapter show that the rising banked population and rapid card growth correlate with VAT-to-GDP increases from 2002 to 2015. One reason for these correlations, we posit, is that a rising level of consumption is shifting from informal (harder to tax) markets to formal (easier to tax) markets as cash use declines and card use grows. Statistical correlations aside, other evidence supports our assumption; for example, rising electronic payments that substitute for cash can explain improved VAT compliance—the Argentine VAT noncompliance rate averaged 36.4% between 2000 and 2005, but it dropped to 20.5% between 2006 and 2010 (Trigueros et al. 2013). No evidence supports conventional VAT compliance arguments such as new bureaucratic reforms and professionalization efforts, rate changes, extension to new products or perhaps an attitudinal or "tax morality" shift—indeed, a general consensus holds that these factors deteriorated after 2002!

Argentina's VAT dependence arose in the context of the 1980s debt crisis and IMF structural adjustment conditionality of the 1990s (Ebrill et al. 2001; Mahon 2004; Tanzi 2007; Bird and Gendron 2007;

Keen and Lockwood 2010). Its VAT ratio resembles a roller-coaster ride: low in the 1970s and 1980s, higher in the 1990s, lower before and after a sovereign default in 2001 and higher (indeed historic highs) for more than a decade. Changes in commodity prices, VAT rates and imports are three common explanations for why the Argentine VAT ratio varies (see Lustig and McLeod 2009; Cetrangolo and Sabaini 2009). Starting in 2010, the commodity market tanked in Argentina, its imports slacked and its economy slowed; again, these three factors should have led to decreases in the VAT ratio, but instead, we saw record increases. Our research findings show that the rising VAT ratio from 2003 to 2015 is the result of four VAT-specific domestic factors: (1) *government policies and financial inclusion*, (2) *financial intermediaries*, (3) *retailers*, and (4) *consumers*.

Government policies influenced VAT revenue by restricting cash withdrawals and notes in circulation and by embracing financial inclusion that required public pension checks, public employee checks and anti-poverty conditional cash transfer (CCT) checks (CCTs ballooned between 2002 and 2015) to be directly deposited into individual bank accounts. No bank account, no check. As a result, the banked population grew over 115% between 2002 and 2015.

Financial intermediaries center on the domestic banking system. International financial market exile threatened domestic banks, a fact the government was well aware of; political scientists refer to such dramatic moments as "critical junctures" and economists often use the term "hard (rather than soft) budget constraints." In short, low tax revenue was no longer an option after 2002. If domestic credit flows dried up, the negative consequences to domestic small and medium enterprises (SMEs) plus larger producers would be profound. And reckless printing of pesos invited a return to the traumatic inflation rates of the early 1990s. Direct deposit channeled sizeable and regular revenue to the banks and in a manner that encouraged the government's goal of peso-use over dollar use. More Argentines with bank accounts allowed banks to offer more credit cards and debit cards. Big box stores such as Coto and Jumbo as well as iconic domestic retailors such as Freddo soon incentivized customers to use cards over cash to increase their sales and security. Consumer behavior regarding card transactions marks a sharp contrast between the 1990s and the post-2002 period. Today, card schemes and card-related quota payment schemes are ubiquitous in

Argentina, especially in and around Buenos Aires. This outcome is curious since Argentina adopted radical financial liberalization policies in the 1990s (low card use) and the precise opposite after 2002 (high card use).

Finally, consumers now spend considerably more with credit cards and debit cards. In addition to retailor and bank incentives, high inflation provides another incentive for card use; customers with credit cards can defer payments and save some money. Also, for larger household purchases, cards are more convenient and safer than cash. As a percentage of total consumption from 2007 to 2015, the critical period in this case study, cash use *decreased* 7.7% (likely reducing informal spending, which is harder to tax), but credit card spending *increased* 14.8% (from 46 to 52.8%) and debit card spending *increased* 16% (from 2.5 to 2.9%). VAT revenue is bound to remain Argentina's main source of public revenue, and current and proposed tax policy initiatives—importantly, the IMF's conditionality in 2019[4]—indicate that VAT dependence is set to rise in the future.

Our analysis uses tax data from the OECD (2017) between 1990 and 2015 as well as consumer transaction data from Euromonitor International (2017) and the World Bank (2017). In the OECD data, revenue from various tax categories oscillate after 1990 (see Fig. 2.1), but VAT-to-GDP remains higher than all other tax categories. In addition, as Argentina's economy stagnated due to commodity price declines starting in 2010, well-known Argentine tax analysts expected (as occurred in the 1990s) that the VAT ratio would fall (Tanzi 2007; Lustig and McLeod 2009). Instead, despite a global commodity price bust, VAT collections increased consistently and broke through the historical high set in the late 1990s. In short, the VAT ratio became counter-cyclical. No significant changes in VAT rates or rules occurred after 2002, and, in fact, rates fell for certain grocery items in 2006.

[4]Argentina's historic September 2018 agreement with the IMF for a record $57 billion calls on the government to reduce the budget deficit from its current 2.9 to 0% of GDP in 2019. Public spending cuts occurred in 2016 and 2017, including layoffs of 33,700 state workers and major cuts to utility subsidies, meaning it is tough to see how IMF conditionality is met without a major boost in tax revenue. Export taxes, slashed in January 2016, were reintroduced in June 2018 in consultations with the IMF, but the scale of revenue that will be needed must come from VAT. Neither the IMF nor the Macri government desires higher corporate or income taxes, as the IMF loan and program are tied to attracting foreign investment, and lots of it.

A general VAT rate of 21% is applied on products, services and imports, but not on exports (Japan alone applies VAT to exports). Bread, water and milk are exempt from VAT, and other basics have a 10.5% VAT rate. Excise taxes are applied to a range of products (tobacco, wines, soft drinks, cosmetics, jewelry, etc.) at rates ranging from 8 to 20%—tobacco (60%) is an exception.

Surprisingly, import restrictions on consumer goods that stifled economic growth after 2010 did not reduce overall VAT revenue—*the opposite occurred*. VAT revenue collected at the customs house as a percentage of total VAT revenue dropped from 42% in 2008 to 28% in 2015, meaning the historic overall VAT ratio gains in this period must have resulted from *internal* VAT collection. The puzzle is how this occurred in a context of stagnant household consumption, flat economic growth and unchanged VAT rates.

Financial Inclusion and VAT

Financial inclusion contributed to counter-cyclical VAT gains. Between 2002 and 2016, credit card ownership increased 735% (6.8–57.4 million) with upper- and middle-income adults obtaining multiple cards linked to various banks and retailers, and debit card ownership increased by 297% (9.7–38.6 million) with each debit card unlike a credit card linked to a specific bank account. Financial inclusion, in short, took place on a massive scale as only adults can obtain credit and debit cards in this country of 44 million people. In addition, from 2002 to 2016, the retail value of the amount charged by consumers (adjusted for inflation) increased 434% in real terms (from US$207 per capita to US$1107 per capita), and the number of card transactions dramatically increased 2690% (from 300 million to over 8.4 billion). Transactions on this scale point to consumers using cards for daily purchases (such as food) that in the past would have been made in cash. Increased card use and ownership suggest that financial inclusion shifted some consumption from informal markets (cash-based and harder to tax) to formal markets (more electronic payments, thus easier to tax). And to tie these financial inclusion trends to the above comments, shifts from informal to formal consumption are one plausible reason for how VAT became counter-cyclical, that is, how the economy can slow down, imports can be restricted and the consumption-to-GDP ratio can be flat but the VAT-to-GDP ratio can still rise.

VAT in Argentina

> Despite its name, the VAT is not generally intended to be a tax on value added as such: rather it is usually intended as a tax on consumption. (Ebrill et al. 2001: 1)

Developing countries that rely primarily on commodity exports typically lack robust manufacturing or value-added industries, which results in VAT falling largely on final formal (not informal) consumption.[5] Argentina fits this description since much of its VAT revenue has been traditionally collected at the custom's house on imported consumer goods (Canterbery 1983; Tanzi 2007, Ch. X). For example, big box stores Jumbo or Coto pay VAT on imported consumer goods (e.g., Johnson and Johnson shampoo or LG televisions).

South American countries introduced VAT ahead of other developing regions. In 1967, Brazil was the first country outside of Europe to adopt a VAT, where it originated after World War II (see Bird and Gendron 2007). Argentina (in 1975) and Chile (in 1975) followed suit. In 1975, Argentina's VAT replaced a host of retail sales taxes that appeared in the 1930s when traditional trade tax revenue collapsed. As a percentage of total tax revenue, retail sales taxes accounted for 19.3% in 1966, and VAT accounted for 19.0% in 1978 and 18.9% in 1985 before virtually collapsing in 1989 (World Bank 1987). VAT in Brazil and Chile also replaced retail sales taxes yet as a percentage of total tax revenue the ratios in these countries climbed in the 1970s and 1980s.

Mahon (2004) links VAT adoption across South America between 1977 and 1995 to the region's chronic struggle to tame inflation; additional tax revenue from VAT was intended to slow down the printing of currency to cover budget deficits. In Argentina, however, VAT yielded negligible revenue in the 1970s and the 1980s, a period of high inflation. Argentine tax policy succumbed to general dysfunction due to an adverse domestic political environment: a traumatic military coup in 1976 was followed by the chaotic Dirty War (1976–1982). A more stable environment surfaced as the country returned to democracy under

[5] Boadway and Sato (2008) note that those who favor trade taxes over VAT stress the fact that the latter does not tax informal consumption, which can incentivize less formal consumption. In turn, trade taxes are easier to collect and harder to skirt (see Emran and Stiglitz 2005).

President Alfonsin (1983–1989), but his term was cut short by a hyperinflationary crisis. Bird (1992) observes, "The base of the Argentine VAT had been badly eroded since its introduction in 1975 by administrative deficiencies regarding small taxpayers and by legislative giveaways to large taxpayers, especially some extremely ill-conceived and costly regional incentives."

After the Alfonsin government collapsed in 1989, incoming President Menem (1989–2000), a Peronist and an ex-provincial governor started tax reforms centered on broadening VAT (Bird 1992: 19). In 1990, two tax reforms (in January and September) significantly broadened the VAT base by adding agricultural products and additional services (Bird 1992; World Bank 1993).[6] Exempt categories fell from 264 to just a handful (Eaton 2002: 146), and the standard VAT rate was raised from 13% (January 1990) to 17% (February 1991) to 18% (July 1991) and eventually to 21% (1995)—where it remains at present. Businesses registered in the VAT system due to broadening reforms more than tripled from 218,036 in 1989 to 931,346 in 1992 (Eaton 2002, Table 5.5). Controversially, starting in 1990, foodstuffs, the largest component of household consumption, were no longer exempt except for water, milk and bread. To put this period in perspective, the percentage of GDP covered by the VAT system jumped from 52.2% in 1989 to 80.0% in 1992, a move that largely accounts for tax-to-GDP jumping from 12.7% in 1989 to 22.5% in 1992. A World Bank report at the time observed: "One of the major achievements has been unambiguously the surge in VAT revenues from 0.6 percent of GDP in the second quarter of 1989 to 9.2 percent of GDP in the fourth quarter of 1992" (World Bank 1993: 4).

VAT-to-GDP during the 1990s peaked around 1998 (at 6.4%) before falling sharply until 2002 (to 3.8%). In 1998, Argentina attempted to reform VAT collection by simplifying the process for small businesses (*monotributo*), but the initiative failed due to rising unemployment and sizable growth in informal (hard to tax) markets at the end of the neoliberal era (Cetrangolo and Sabaini 2009; Frenkel 2006; Tanzi 2007). A large informal sector distinguishes Argentina from industrialized countries and this diminishes the collection of a range of taxes

[6]The 1990 reform follows the recommendations of a World Bank (1989: 67) assessment team in the country in 1989: "The VAT would be generalized to all goods and services, at a uniform rate, which could be the present 15 percent or the 18 percent prevailing until August 1988."

(income, corporate and VAT) (Emran and Stiglitz 2005). Observers agree that Menem's neoliberal policies of the 1990s triggered a swelling of the informal sector that acted as a drag on overall tax collection. With Menem's VAT-oriented tax reforms, fiscal federalism—the original 1975 VAT law stipulates the federal government must share a set percentage of VAT revenue with Argentina's 23 provinces and the city of Buenos Aires—caused further problems in the 1990s. "Each time the national government attempted to raise taxes to reduce the fiscal deficit, about half of the total tax increase went to the provincial governments, which immediately spent all the additional income and often more" (Tanzi 2007: 133). No firm subnational budget constraint exists in Argentina (as there is in the USA, for example), so subnational overspending and federal bailouts of provincial governments occur constantly and strain federal finances (Jones et al. 2000; Nicolini et al. 2002).

Figure 2.1 reveals the composition of Argentine taxation from 1990 to 2015, and it is important to highlight the country's macroeconomic volatility at the start of the 1990s. Argentina's high inflation between 1989 and 1991 peaked at around 20,000 percent, and in this volatile climate, tax-to-GDP remained low even by Argentine standards and it left the country below the regional average. However, once inflation dropped at the end of 1991, Argentina's tax-to-GDP recovered and peaked in 1993 at 18.1%, a ratio above the regional average. VAT became (and remains) the primary source of tax revenue. Income taxes and corporate taxes are the next two highest sources of tax revenue in Argentina and they each contribute 10% toward total tax revenue—but even combined, they are less than how much tax revenue VAT generates. Export taxes had accounted for almost one-third of federal tax revenue in the 1980s (Deese and Reeder 2008), but rate cuts as part of trade liberalization resulted in export taxes nearly disappearing from 1992 to 2001. In the immediate aftermath of Argentina's default in December 2001, export taxes were raised in 2002—the tax on soybeans increased from 3.5 to 23.5% and the tax on soybean oil increased from 1 to 19.3% (Argentina is the world's largest exporter of soybean oil). By 2005, export taxes accounted for 8.6% of total tax revenue (Melo 2007; Lustig and McLeod 2009; Richardson 2009; Fairfield 2011; Kaufman 2011; Lustig and Pessino 2012; World Bank 2013).

In 2007, Tanzi (2007: 149) foresaw Argentina's elevated tax burden as unsustainable and bound to reverse quickly: "I would be surprised and pleased if the current fiscal situation were maintained, but I fear that

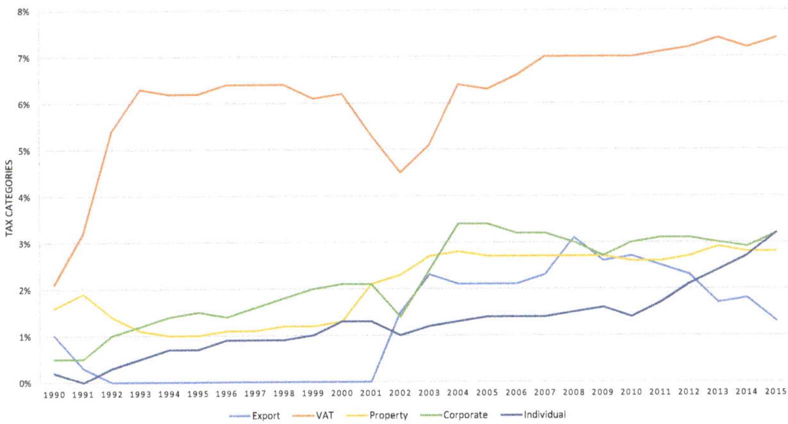

Fig. 2.2 Selected tax revenue categories as a percentage of GDP for Argentina, 1990–2015 (*Source* OECD [2017])

this will be difficult." Later accounts by the IMF's Lustig and McLeod (2009), Cetrangolo and Sabaini (2009) as well as Kaufman (2011) concur that Argentina's tax-to-GDP ratio would fall along with commodity prices. Yet, after the commodity boom ended in 2010, tax-to-GDP continued to rise.

As shown in Fig. 2.2, VAT revenue continued to rise even after the 2010 commodity bust resulted in lower household consumption and a general economic slowdown. No changes in VAT rates, thresholds or exemptions can explain this outcome. As shown in Fig. 2.3, household consumption-to-GDP and VAT moved together from 1993 to 2003. Less clear is why after 2003, household consumption increased only 1.7% (64.33–65.45%) while VAT-to-GDP increased 15.6% (reaching an historic high of 7.4% in 2015).

In Fig. 2.4, we see that VAT from imports varied from a high of 45% to a low of 26.4% from 1996 to 2015. VAT-to-GDP generally follows the trend of total value of VAT from imports until around 2009, then it starts to diverge. VAT from internal sources grew 7% from 2009 to 2015 and VAT-to-GDP grew 5.7% while VAT from imports shrank 14.4%. Our argument, detailed in the following section, is that more VAT revenue was generated domestically (internally) due to an increase in the use of electronic payments.

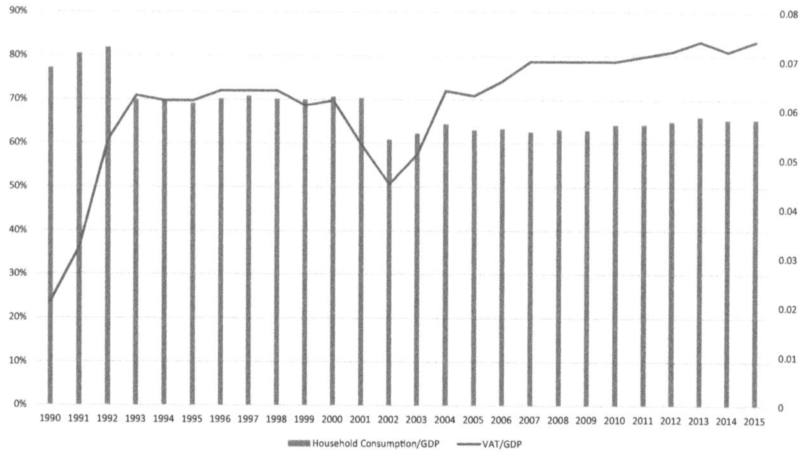

Fig. 2.3 Household consumption-to-GDP (left *y*-axis) and VAT revenue-to-GDP (right *y*-axis) in Argentina, 1990–2015 (*Source* OECD [2017])

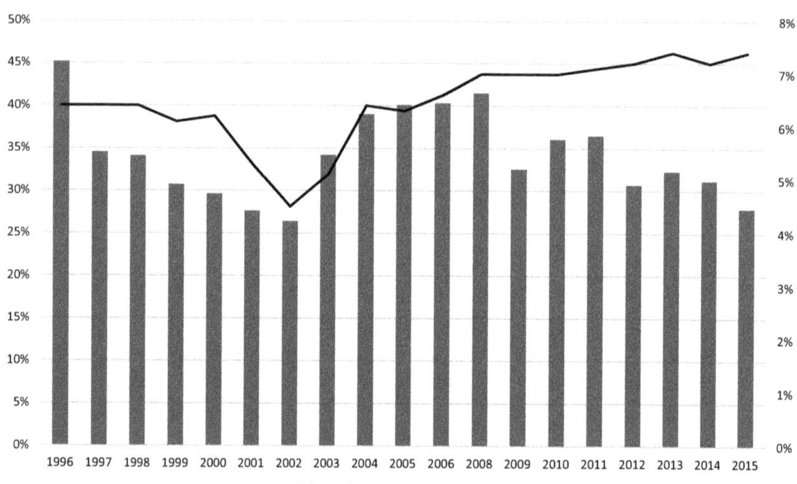

Fig. 2.4 VAT from imports as a percentage of total VAT revenue (left-hand *y*-axis) and VAT-to-GDP, 1996–2015 (the year 2007 is eliminated due to incomplete data) (*Source* Central Bank of Argentina)

Pesos to Plastic—Consumer Markets and VAT Post-2002 Argentina

> [J]ust as true paper money arises out of the function of money as the circulating medium, so does money-credit take root spontaneously in the function of money as the means of payment. (Marx 1990: 224)

Argentina's rapid growth in the number of people with bank accounts and how this corresponded to an increase in the issuance and use of credit cards and debit cards need further explanation. The percentage of Argentines with a bank account went from 41.6% in 2003 to 89.6% in 2016 (an increase of 115.4%) (Euromonitor International 2017). Two key factors explain how the Argentine government shepherded more people into the banking system. First, while the Central Bank of the Republic of Argentina in 1997 passed a provision requiring most payrolls to be filtered through the formal banking system using direct deposit, the measure was not in fact enforced until after 2002, when the government was scrambling to stabilize the economy after abandoning the one-to-one Peso-to-US Dollar peg (Economist Intelligence Unit 2005: 13). After the peso was decoupled, it experienced a significant devaluation, so the payroll deposit policy helped to get people back into the banking system after 2002. Financial inclusion by way of this direct deposit payroll policy was impressive; focusing on public sector payrolls—roughly 25% of total employment in 2015—the Labor Ministry estimates that a sizeable public workforce of 240,600 federal employees and 2,284,000 provincial employees all received salaries via direct deposit arrangements with banks.

Second, anti-poverty CCT programs and pensions joined payrolls—again, no bank account, no monthly check. Argentina had no CCT programs prior to 2002—Mexico adopted the region's first national CCT program in 1997 and Brazil followed suit in 2002. However, Argentina's Universal Child Allowance (UCA), a CCT program targeting poor and informal sector households grew rapidly to the point that by 2010, it covered 28.8% of children under 18. Also, because UCA delivers a larger monthly cash stipend than comparable CCT programs in Brazil (Bolsa Familia) or Mexico (Progresa), its effect was more redistributive and its boost to the consumption of poor households was stronger. Other Argentine CCT programs covered a further 7% of the population. No Latin American country expanded CCT programs faster than

Argentina between 2005 (1.12 million people) and 2010 (11.79 million people). Linking CCT growth to financial inclusion, Argentina began with "zero" CCT-linked bank accounts among poor and informal sector households in 2002; yet, the total jumped to a quarter of the country's total population by 2010. Pension coverage grew as well. Argentina expanded pension coverage by renationalizing pensions in 2008 (reversing the privatization of the 1990s) and in a controversial move extended pension coverage to informal workers in 2012. In 2005, a total of 30% of retirees had no access to the pension system; however, the figure dropped to 10% by 2012 and today, Argentina possesses the highest coverage in Latin America. To summarize, after 2002, monthly direct deposit of payrolls, CCTs and pension payments explains how Argentina's banked population jumped from 41.6% in 2003 to 89.6% in 2016.

More people in the banking system meant, among other things, that banks could offer more financial products—especially credit cards and debit cards. As a result, Fig. 2.5 shows a 735% increase in credit card ownership rates between 2002 and 2016 (from 6.9 to 57.4 million) and an increase of 296% for debit cards (from 9.7 to 38.6 million) over

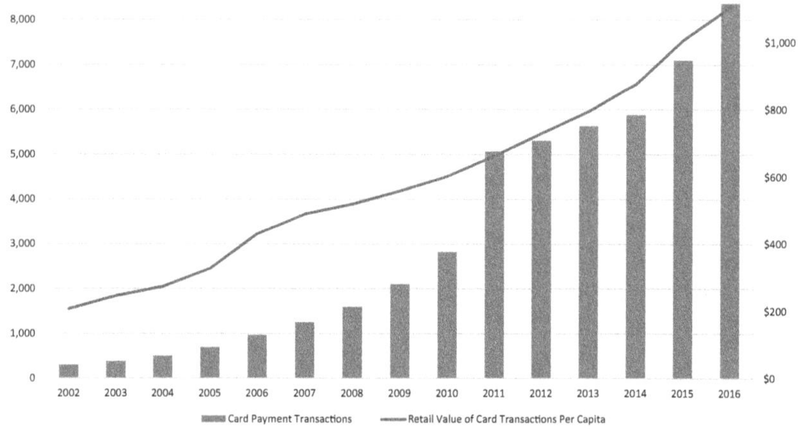

Fig. 2.5 Growth in credit cards, debit cards (measured in thousands on the left *y*-axis) and the percentage of banked population (right *y*-axis) in Argentina, 2002–2016 (*Source* Euromonitor International [2017])

the same period. The growing circulation of credit cards and debit cards, as well as the significant rise in the number of card transactions and value of total card transactions, is a contributing factor to rising VAT revenue since 2002.

But the government went beyond incentivizing card ownership. In 2001, the government started a policy to give a 5% VAT discount on debit card purchases. "The rationale behind the move [in 2001] was that it would help boost the use of bank products in the country where checks are a rarity and where cash is typically preferred over credit and debit cards or other means of payment" (Bloomberg 2017). The Central Bank further accelerated the growth in cards by giving a discount on VAT taxes for purchases made using credit cards and debit cards (Economist Intelligence Unit 2005: 14). For example, Coto Hypermarket (a large supermarket retailer in Argentina) gave 15% discounts on purchases from Tuesday to Thursday made using credit cards. In response, Argentines, many of whom had never had access to credit before, became willing customers. The Central Bank has tried various ways to shift more informal cash transactions into formal markets. Most of these attempts have failed, and a common argument for these failings is that informal markets are a function of poor Argentine tax administration and enforcement (Bergman 2003).

Our findings suggest that regardless of changes in tax administration and enforcement performance, the Argentine government found the right mix of policies that increased formal banking participation and led to more consumer credit and electronic payments (perhaps by decreasing informal market activities). Argentina's high-inflation environment (ranging roughly between 20 and 40% between 2013 and 2018) has also helped to increase credit card use since payment can be deferred into the future, and if paid in full and on time, borrowers benefit from the float, that is, buying now and paying later with cheaper Pesos. Card users also get any available VAT tax discounts and incentives provided by the credit card and debit card companies.

In recent years, some public opinion polls list personal security concerns ahead of inflation as the country's most pressing problem. Up to 2016, the 100-peso note was the largest cash note despite inflation increasing to around 25%. People feel uncomfortable carrying around substantial amounts of cash if they are going to make an expensive or moderately expensive purchase, but credit cards and debit cards work just as well, are convenient and grant people peace of mind. Also, stolen cash will not be reimbursed, whereas credit cards and debit cards have borrower protections that limit potential personal financial loss. ATM machines limited cash withdrawals per visit between 2002 and 2015—the 2015 limit in pesos was roughly equivalent to US$135. People could visit multiple ATMs, but this was time-consuming. Finally, ATM machines, especially in Buenos Aires, often ran out of pesos over weekends and holidays.

Retailers are acknowledging (in some cases encouraging) customers' increasing preference for using credit cards and debit cards. While there is a cost to retailers for accepting credit and debit cards, it is not a zero-sum game and both retailers and consumers benefit. Retailers in Argentina benefit from increased card use in several ways. First, the number of point-of-sale terminals (POS—i.e., the electronic box needed to swipe a client's card) in Argentina increased 94.7% (678,600 to over 1.3 million) from 2004 to 2016 (Euromonitor International 2017). Retailers have known for many decades that when customers use cards, they spend more money (see Feinberg 1986). Lewis Mandell (1990) documents that the first credit cards were issued by retailers and gasoline stations in the early twentieth century to boost sales. Second, with Argentines limited in how many Pesos they could withdraw each day between 2002 and 2015, retailers that only rely on cash might see lower sales, especially for more moderate to expensive items. Also, after 2001, Argentina had hard currency restrictions that squeezed retailers that relied on cash—likely compelling more of them to accept cards. Third, same as customers, retailers preferred not to have significant amounts of cash around for security reasons. Accepting credit cards and debit cards minimized this risk and fear. Fourth, retailers can raise their prices to pass the merchant fees for processing cards onto consumers, which invariably leads to some inflation, but it is small when added to all other prices paid by households.

Figure 2.6 shows that the total annual retail value of credit card and debit card transactions per capita (adjusted for inflation) increased 434% ($207–$1105) from 2002 to 2016, and almost all of this growth occurred after 2005. Also, Argentines are using their credit cards and debit cards for a larger percentage of purchases. Card spending as a ratio of total personal consumption increased 214% from 1999 to 2013 (from 8.4 to 26.4%). By 2013, over one-quarter of all consumer purchases were made with either a credit card or debit card.

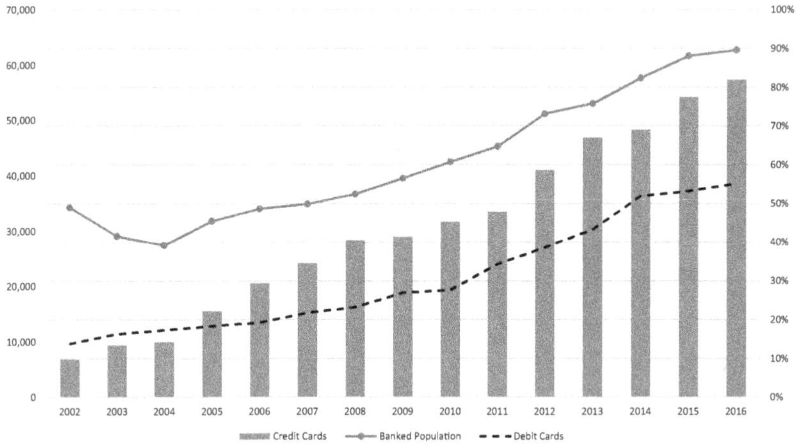

Fig. 2.6 Number of credit card and debit card (i.e., card) payment transactions in millions of 2016 US Dollars (right-hand, *y*-axis) and total value of all card payment transactions in retail value-to-GDP (left-hand *y*-axis) (*Source* Euromonitor International [2017])

And the increase in the use of cards has occurred at the same time as a decrease in the use of cash and checks (Euromonitor International 2017). So, most Argentines are not necessarily spending more money because of their access to consumer credit; they are merely using a different spending mechanism. Data from the Central Bank of Argentina (2014) show that a large majority of consumer credit purchases are made without incurring interest charges and over 80% of credit card balances are paid in full each month. Most Argentine households are using credit cards to reduce inflation costs, take advantage of VAT discounts, and increase the safety and efficiency of how they spend their money.

Empirical Analysis

We now analyze the relationship between VAT-to-GDP and the size of the banked population and credit card and debit card ownership and use. Card data are from Euromonitor International (2017); VAT-to-GDP data is from OECD (2017); and imports-to-GDP and agriculture-to-GDP are from the World Bank (2017).

Two control variables are standard in studies about VAT (see Aizenman and Jinjarak 2005): (a) Agriculture-to-GDP, which we expect to be negative because the larger the agricultural sector relative to GDP, the less the tax collections; and (b) imports-to-GDP, which we expect to be positive since a large portion of VAT comes from import duties.

We estimate five contemporaneous (static) time series models using OLS regression. Since our data are annual, we do not expect lagged effects—i.e., the data are stationary. We use Durbin-Watson statistics to test for autocorrelation—and in all models, there is no presence of positive or negative autocorrelation.

The dependent variable is Value-Added Tax Revenue-to-GDP (VAT/GDP) in Argentina. We test five different independent variables of interest: (1) the percent of the banked population; (2) the number of cards (credit and debit cards) owned per-capita; (3) the number of card transactions per-capita; (4) the log of real credit card spending per-capita; and (5) the percentage of total credit card spending-to-total household spending. The time period for the data is 2002–2015—except Model 5 that covers 2007–2015.[7] The baseline model is the following:

$$\frac{\text{VAT}}{\text{GDP}_t} = \beta_0 + \beta_1 \frac{\text{Imports}}{\text{GDP}_t} + \beta_2 \frac{\text{Agriculture}}{\text{GDP}_t} + \upsilon_t$$

In Table 2.1, we see that in all five models, Agriculture-to-GDP is negative and significant and Imports-to-GDP is positive and significant, which matches what is found in the literature (Aizenman and Jinjarak 2005). Looking at Model 1, as the percentage of the population with a bank account increased in Argentina from 2002 to 2015, the VAT-to-GDP ratio also increased. A one percent increase in the banked population is correlated with a 0.033% increase in VAT-to-GDP—e.g., a one percent increase in the banked population in 2015 would equate to around $200 million (in 2015 US dollars) in extra VAT revenue, *ceteris paribus*. Model 2 shows that as the number of cards per-capita owned by Argentines increases, so does the VAT-to-GDP ratio. Each additional card per-capita increase resulted in a 1.035% increase in the VAT-to-GDP ratio—e.g., one extra card per-person (roughly 43.4 million extra cards)

[7] Data on card ownership are only available annually and start in 2002. Card spending data are also annual and are available starting in 2007. Therefore, our models are limited to sample sizes of 14 (years) for models 1–4 and 8 (years) for model 5.

Table 2.1 Time series regressions: sample period 2002–2015 annually (model 5 period is 2007–2015)

	Model 1	*Model 2*	*Model 3*	*Model 4*	*Model 5*
Intercept	3.11*	3.919***	3.746***	1.459	0.244
	(2.08)	(4.21)	(3.61)	(1.04)	(0.15)
% banked population	0.033***				
	(3.88)				
Cards owned per-capita		1.035***			
		(5.61)			
Card transactions per-capita			0.106***		
			(5.15)		
Log credit card spending				0.717***	
				(5.29)	
Credit card spending-to-total household spending					0.125***
					(4.92)
Agriculture-to-GDP	−0.338***	−0.267***	−0.243***	−0.256***	−0.264**
	(−4.80)	(−4.39)	(−3.47)	(−3.88)	(−3.72)
Imports-to-GDP	0.287***	0.242***	0.227***	0.221***	0.182**
	(6.11)	(7.74)	(7.00)	(7.02)	(3.31)
Durbin–Watson	1.80	1.975	1.816	1.623	2.761
R^2	0.94	0.96	0.94	0.96	0.92
F-test	49.16***	83.64***	73.10***	76.30***	19.65***

Notes *, **, and *** denote significance at the 10, 5, and 1% levels, respectively; *t*-statistics are in parentheses. Dependent variable is Argentina's Value-Added Tax Revenue-to-Gross Domestic Product would add over $6 billion in extra VAT revenue, *ceteris paribus*. Models 3–5 show that as card spending increased, so did VAT revenue.

There are a few explanations for our results. The first possibility is that increased card use resulted in more spending (above aggregate income) and this boosted aggregate demand resulting in more VAT revenue (see Zandi et al. 2013). However, we know from Fig. 2.2 above that consumption-to-GDP has been flat. Also, consumer debt levels in Argentina have not changed in many years according to data from Argentina's Central Bank (2014).

A second explanation is that there was a change in VAT rates or VAT enforcement. We know VAT rates did not change over this period and there appear to be no changes in VAT enforcement.

A third explanation is that because people are using more cards, they have shifted some of their spending from informal markets that are hard to tax to formal markets that are easier to tax. We believe that this is a plausible explanation for a few reasons. First, from 2007 to 2015, cash use as a percentage of total consumption decreased by 7.7% in Argentina, whereas credit card consumption rose 14.8% as a percentage of total consumption and debit card consumption rose 2.9%. Second, the VAT noncompliance rate averaged 36.4% between 2000 and 2005 and fell to 20.5% between 2006 and 2010 (Trigueros et al. 2013). Also, Bertranou et al. (2014: 16) found that the rate of non-registered employees (i.e., informal) fell from 49.1% in 2003 to 34.5% in 2011, which is almost a 30% reduction of the informal workforce.

Conclusions

VAT revenue is responsible for one-quarter of Argentina's total tax revenue, which is its largest tax category. Argentina's VAT-to-GDP ratio has risen to historic highs, and by 2015, the country stood as a high tax-to-GDP country (the highest in Latin America starting in 2015), a break from its historical norm. Previous research has emphasized commodity prices, interest rates, imports and economic performance as factors affecting VAT revenue. In Argentina, however, the commodity boom ended around 2011, economic growth slowed and imports shrank, which should have resulted in sharp decreases in VAT-to-GDP, but the opposite occurred. VAT-to-GDP continued to rise and surpass historic highs. Our research stressing financial inclusion finds that the banked population in Argentina increased significantly after 2002 due to the enforcement of a policy that deposited paychecks for public employees, pensioners and anti-poverty cash recipients into banks. Consequently, Argentina's banked population rose from 41.6% in 2003 to 89.6% in 2016 (an increase of 115.4%). As a result of financial inclusion, credit card and debit card ownership and use also increased. Using time series regression, we found that each 1% increase in the banked population resulted in a 0.033% increase in VAT-to-GDP. In addition, for each one card increase in the amount of cards per-capita resulted in a 1.04% increase in VAT-to-GDP. Credit card spending is also associated with higher levels of VAT-to-GDP. Given all the possible explanations for why VAT-to-GDP would continue to rise amid falling commodity prices, falling imports, flat consumption and economic growth, we believe that financial inclusion and rising card use has shifted some consumption from informal markets that are difficult to tax to more formal markets that are easier to tax.

References

Acemoglu, D., and J. Robinson. 2012. *Why Nations Fail, the Origins of Power, Prosperity, and Poverty*. New York: Crown Business.

Aizenman, J., and Y. Jinjarak. 2005. "The Collection Efficiency of the Value Added Tax: Theory and International Experience." NBER Working Paper 11539. http://www.nber.org/papers/w11539.

Bergman, M. S. 2003. "Tax Reforms and Tax Compliance: The Divergent Paths of Chile and Argentina." *Journal of Latin American Studies* 35 (3): 593–624.

Bertranou, F., L. Casanova, M. Jimenez, and M. Jimenez. 2014. *Informality and Employment Quality in Argentina: Country Case Study on Labour Market Segmentation*. www.ilo.org/wcmsp5/groups/public/—ed_protect/—protrav/—travail/documents/publication/wcms_313839.pdf.

Bird, R. M. 1992. "Tax Reform in Latin America: A Review of Some Recent Experiences." *Latin American Research Review* 27 (1): 7–36.

Bird, R. M., and P. P. Gendron. 2007. *The VAT in Developing and Transitional Countries*. Cambridge: Cambridge University Press.

Bloomberg. 2017. "Argentina Ends 5 Percent VAT Rebate on Debit Cards." January 6.

Boadway, R., and M. Sato. 2008. "Optimal Tax Design and Enforcement with an Informal Sector." Queen's Economics Department Working Paper No. 1168, Kingston, ON.

Brautigam, D., O. Fjeldstad, and M. Moore. 2008. *Taxation and State-Building in Developing Countries, Capacity and Consent*. New York: Cambridge University Press.

Calvert, S., and P. Calvert. 1989. *Argentina: Political Culture and Instability.* London: Macmillan.

Canterbery, E. R. 1983. "Tax Reform and Incomes Policy: A VATIP Proposal." *Journal of Post Keynesian Economics* 5 (3): 430–439.

Central Bank of the Argentine Republic. 2014. *Consolidated Balance Sheets of the Financial System.* www.google.com/url?sa=t&rct=j&q=&esrc=s&source=web&cd=1&ved=0CCcQFjAA&url=http%3A%2F%2Fwww.bcra.gov.ar%2Fpdfs%2Festadistica%2Fbaldethis.xls&ei=6_aEU5uuMcbJsQTIo4DYCg&usg=AFQjCNEVmhq49SATyCuoZvkPKDVoisrApg&sig2=08b2PTV3bSd9t5hSDK1EOQ&bvm=bv.67720277,d.cWc.

Cetrangolo, O., and J. C. G. Sabaini. 2009. "Tax Policy in Argentina: Between Solvency and Emergency." Initiative for Policy Dialogue Working Paper Series, Columbia University, October.

Cortés Conde, R. 2013. *The Political Economy of Argentina in the Twentieth Century.* Cambridge: Cambridge University Press.

Deese, W., and J. Reeder. 2008. "Export Taxes on Agricultural Products: Recent History and Economic Modeling of Soya Bean Export Taxes in Argentina." *Journal of International Commerce and Trade* 1: 185.

Di Tella, G., and R. Dornbusch. 1989. *The Political Economy of Argentina, 1946–1983.* Pittsburgh: University of Pittsburgh Press.

Eaton, K. 2002. *Politicians and Economic Reform in New Democracies: Argentina and the Philippines in the 1990s.* University Park: Penn State Press.

Ebrill, L., M. Keen, J. P. Bodin, and V. Summers. 2001. *The Modern VAT.* Washington, DC: IMF.

Economist Intelligence Unit. 2005. *Assessing Payments Systems in Latin America.* http://graphics.eiu.com/files/ad_pdfs/eiu_visa_eng_wp.pdf.

Emran, S., and J. Stiglitz. 2005. "On Selective Indirect Tax Reform in Developing Countries." *Journal of Public Economics* 89 (4): 599–623.

Euromonitor International. 2017. *Argentina Statistics.* Retrieved from Euromonitor Passport GMID Database.

Fairfield, T. 2011. "Business Power and Protest: Argentina's Agricultural Producers Protest in Comparative Context." *Studies in Comparative International Development* 46 (4): 424–453.

Feinberg, R. 1986. "Credit Cards as Spending Facilitating Stimuli: A Conditioning Interpretation." *Journal of Consumer Research* 13 (3): 348–356.

Frenkel, R. 2006. "An Alternative to Inflation Targeting in Latin America: Macroeconomic Policies Focused on Employment." *Journal of Post Keynesian Economics* 28 (4): 573–591.

Jones, M., P. Sanguinetti, and M. Tommasi. 2000. "Politics, Institutions, and Fiscal Performance in a Federal System: An Analysis of the Argentine Provinces." *Journal of Development Economics* 61: 305–333.

Kaufman, R. 2011. "The Political Left, the Export Boom, and the Populist Temptation." In *The Resurgence of the Latin American Left*, ed. S. Levitsky and K. Roberts. Baltimore: Johns Hopkins Press.

Keen, M., and B. Lockwood. 2010. "The Value Added Tax: Its Causes and Consequences." *Journal of Development Economics* 92 (2): 138–151.

Levi, M. 1988. *Of Rule and Revenue*. Berkeley: University of California Press.

Lustig, N., and D. McLeod. 2009. *Are Latin America's New Left Regimes Reducing Inequality Faster?* Washington, DC: Woodrow Wilson Center for International Scholars, Latin American Program (July).

Lustig, N., and C. Pessino. 2012. "Social Spending and Income Redistribution in Argentina During the 2000s: The Rising Role of Noncontributory Pensions." Serie Documentos de Trabajo, Universidad del CEMA, Área: economía, No. 499.

Mahon, J. 2004. "Causes of Tax Reform in Latin America, 1977–1995." *Latin American Research Review* 39 (1): 3–30.

Mandell, L. 1990. *The Credit Card Industry: A History*. Ann Arbor: University of Michigan.

Marx, K. 1990. *Capital: Volume 1*. London: Penguin Books.

Melo, M. A. 2007. "Institutional Weakness and the Puzzle of Argentina's Low Taxation." *Latin American Politics and Society* 49 (4): 115–148.

Migdal, J. 1988. *Strong Societies and Weak States, State-Society Relations and State Capabilities in the Third World*. Princeton: Princeton University Press.

Nicolini, J. P., J. Posadas, J. Sanguinetti, P. Sanguinetti, and M. Tommasi. 2002. "Decentralization, Fiscal Discipline in Sub-National Governments and the Bailout Problem: The Case of Argentina." Inter-American Development Bank Research Network Working Paper.

North, D., and R. P. Thomas. 1973. *The Rise of the Western World, A New Economic History*. Cambridge: Cambridge University Press.

OECD. 2017. "Revenue Statistics in Latin America: Comparative Tables." OECD. stats.oecd.org/Index.aspx?DataSetCode=RSLACT#.

Richardson, N. P. 2009. "Export-Oriented Populism: Commodities and Coalitions in Argentina." *Studies in Comparative International Development* 44 (3): 228–255.

Rock, D. 1987. *Argentina 1516–1987: From Spanish Colonization to Alfonsín*. Berkeley: University of California Press.

Steinmo, S. 1993. *Taxation & Democracy*. New Haven: Yale University Press.

Tanzi, V. 2007. *Argentina: An Economic Chronicle*. New York: Pinto Books.

Teera, J., and J. Hudson. 2004. "Tax Performance: A Comparative Study." *Journal of International Development* 16 (6): 785–802.

TheGlobalEconomy. 2018. "Government Spending as a Percent of GDP." https://www.theglobaleconomy.com/.

Trigueros, M., F. Longinotti, and J. Vecorena. 2013. "Estimating Tax Noncompliance in Latin America: 2000–2010." International Tax Compact. www.taxcompact.net/documents/ITC_2013-05_Estimating-tax-non-compliance-in-LAC.pdf.

World Bank. 1987. "The Argentinean Experience with the Value-Added Tax." World Bank Document #DRD235.

World Bank. 1989. "Argentina: Tax Policy for Stabilization and Economic Recovery." World Bank. documents.worldbank.org/curated/en/923791468209363007/pdf/multi-page.pdf.

World Bank. 1993. "Effects of Tax Reform on Argentina's Revenues." WPS 1192.

World Bank. 2013. "Shifting Gears to Accelerated Shared Prosperity in Latin America and the Caribbean." World Bank Document #78507.

World Bank. 2017. "DataBank." World Bank. databank.worldbank.org/data/home.aspx.

Zandi, M., V. Singh, and J. Irving. 2013. *The Impact of Electronic Payments on Economic Growth.* usa.visa.com/download/corporate/_media/moodys-economy-white-paper-feb-2013.pdf.

CHAPTER 3

Financial Inclusion and Value-Added Taxes in Argentina, Brazil and Chile

Abstract This chapter shows how government financial inclusion policies increased bank participation rates in Argentina, Brazil and Chile, and this in turn increased access to (and use of) debt and credit cards. In Argentina and Chile in particular, financial inclusion along with card-based consumption grew drastically and is positively correlated with higher value-added tax (VAT) collection. VAT compliance strengthens at intermediate stages (VAT receipt needed to receive a tax benefit) and weakens at final consumption (VAT receipt garners no value to retailers), yet card transactions occur at this final stage. In recent years, we observe an anomaly where VAT revenue has increased despite unchanged VAT rates and stagnant economies, something we link to more formal and less informal final consumption. Fixed-effects regression is used to test the influence of changes in the banked population, card-based consumption and size of the informal economy on VAT revenue from 2002 to 2015.

Keywords VAT · Consumption · Credit cards · Banking · South America · Informal economy · Shadow economy

Introduction

Dependence on value-added tax (VAT) revenue is common and growing across South America (Gomez-Sabaini and Moran 2014; World Bank 2014; CEPAL 2016). Different than OECD countries, VAT in

K. Mitchell and R. H. Scott, III, *Pesos or Plastic?*,
https://doi.org/10.1007/978-3-030-14876-8_3

South America is an indirect tax on domestic final consumption more than on value added on intermediary stages of production chains, and it generates more public revenue than trade, income, corporate, financial transactions or property taxes. Argentina, Brazil and Chile swapped traditional sales taxes (in the 1960s and 1970s) and later trade taxes (in the 1980s and 1990s) for a broad-based VAT (though Brazil later reinstituted some sales tax). Today, policy-makers weigh swapping income taxes for further reliance on VAT.[1] As discussed in the previous chapter, Argentina has proposed eliminating income taxes altogether, while Brazil and Chile signal sizable income and corporate tax cuts ahead to spur private sector investment and economic growth. Rising VAT dependence creates a need to examine potential factors that impact VAT collection rates, especially when external economic conditions deteriorate, for example, when global interest rates rise and global commodity prices fall (see Mitchell and Scott 2018).

In the region, VAT collection research and debate tend to fall into one of three general categories. The first focuses on the policy choice to switch from taxing trade to taxing consumption. Sales taxes proliferated in the region in the 1930s as world trade collapsed and trade tax revenue along with it (Lindholm 1974; Due 1974). Later, VAT debates in the 1960s and 1970s focused on the benefits of a unified VAT over multiple sales taxes (easy to evade) and cascading taxes (distorted markets) (Sanchez Roman 2012). National VAT systems revolve around an incentive-laden paper trail from the start of production to intermediary production stages to final consumption of goods and services, and it is this extensive paper trail and the inherent incentives it contains to producers, retailors, consumers and auditors that reduce the impulse to evade compared to traditional sales taxes. The IMF spearheaded a new round of consumption tax debates in the 1980s and 1990s, this time tied to the more general goal of neoliberal restructuring (Tanzi 1992; Ebrill et al. 2001; Mahon 2004; Bird and Gendron 2007; Spiller and Tommasi 2007;

[1] Income taxes fall on formal sector workers via payrolls due to the region's high instance of informal employment as well as capital flight among the wealthy. Informal employment in these three highly urban economies includes middle-class services (psycho-analysis, in-home medical visits, etc.,) as well as working-class jobs (street vendors, domestic servants, construction, etc.). Taxing consumption, which takes place disproportionately at the customs house, is seen by some as a more equitable and stable tax base.

Focanti et al. 2016; Hallerberg and Scartascini 2016). In short, foreign debt pressures exposed South American countries to multilateral actors advocating for greater dependence on VAT. This is most obvious in Argentina as it switched to VAT dependence in 1991 that resulted from a World Bank taskforce report from 1989. The move was seen as placing public revenue on a firm tax base (consumption is a larger percentage of GDP than imports and exports), as shielding taxation from boom and bust cycles tied to international commodity prices, and as more attractive to coveted foreign investors.

The second stresses VAT-specific rates, thresholds (size of businesses obliged to pay VAT), exemptions (perhaps food and medicine) and enforcement schemes (Cnossen 1998; Bergman 2003; Keen and Mintz 2004; Bergman and Nevarez 2006; Melo 2007; Artana and Templado 2010; Sanchez 2011). Since taxes are hard to collect and people must be compelled, VAT collection according to many corresponds to the associated incentive structures attached to policy choices over rates, exemptions (i.e., adding food, medicines or services) and enforcement reform (i.e., elite audit teams or education campaigns). Today, debates around new technologies link to consumer behavior as well as mobile-money and e-banking, and how these might impact VAT collection in the future, grew out of earlier debates on rates, thresholds and exemptions.

Finally, the third ties recent VAT revenue gains to a commodity boom (2002–2010) that fueled economic growth and more household consumption (Tanzi 2007; Lustig and McLeod 2009; Mahon 2012; Bird and Zolt 2015). Price rises of exported commodities (i.e., corn, wheat, soya beans and cooking oil in Argentina, soya beans, meat, fruit, coffee, and iron ore in Brazil, and copper in Chile) furnished the hard currency, the tax revenue and the strengthening of local currency that these countries utilized to import more consumer goods and services, which is important because VAT is disproportionately collected in developing countries at the customs house on imports (Ebrill et al. 2001; Azaria and Robinson 2005; Bird and Gendron 2007). In sum, recent VAT research stresses that rising VAT revenue is a by-product of a commodity boom that boosted economic growth, domestic consumption and imports—and, in Argentina (70%), Brazil (64%) and Chile (61%) consumption is the largest component of GDP, so there is a logic to this assumption. This is restating the argument that VAT is pro-cyclical—i.e., matches the performance of the economy.

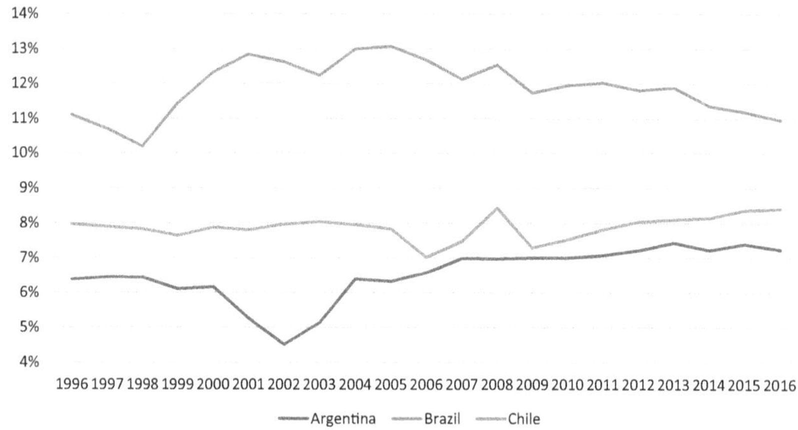

Fig. 3.1 VAT-to-GDP in Argentina, Brazil (with sales taxes) and Chile (1996–2016) (*Source* Authors' calculations using OECD [2018] data)

However, as shown in Fig. 3.1, VAT-to-GDP has remained elevated (i.e., commodity boom levels) in Chile (2009–2016) and in Argentina (2009–2016). VAT/sales taxes-to-GDP remain high despite unchanged VAT rates and exemptions, customary lax enforcement, stagnant economic growth,[2] low commodity prices, falling household consumption, and most counterintuitive annual import totals in US Dollars have trended *down* in Argentina since 2011 and in Chile since 2012. Argentina and Chile present a clear puzzle. As expected, Argentine VAT collected at the customs house as a percentage of total VAT fell sharply after 2011; in 2008 (height of the commodity boom), it stood at 41.5% and in 2015, it decreased to 27.9%. The point to emphasize, VAT revenue measured by VAT-to-GDP continued to be elevated (as explained in Chapter 2) after the commodity boom on the back of domestic collection. Economic growth previously stalled in the late 1990s, a time when Argentina, Brazil and Chile depended on VAT (and sales taxes too, for Brazil) and commodity prices fell (notably for oil), and VAT-to-GDP as anticipated declined. Falling Brazilian VAT revenue (1995–1998) contributed to its 1998–1999 economic crisis and decreases in Argentine

[2]Over the recent four-year period 2012 and 2015, GDP growth averaged 0.38% in Argentina, 0.42% in Brazil and 3.38% in Chile (World Bank 2017).

VAT revenue (1999–2001) contributed to that country's historic sovereign default in December 2001. Argentine VAT-to-GDP in the 1990s peaked around 1998 (at 6.4%) before falling sharply by 2002 (to 3.8%). If VAT had remained at its 1998 level, given that it is Argentina's largest tax revenue stream, much misery and suffering could have been avoided. If South American countries are wedded to VAT dependence, which they appear to be, an urgent need arises to understand how revenue collection can be maintained in a context of weak commodity prices and stagnate economic growth, precisely the conditions found in Argentina, Brazil and Chile after the commodity boom.

We argue a new personal finance phenomenon is occurring in South America, and it has had (and will continue to have) a positive impact on domestic VAT collection (and sales taxes in Brazil) by lowering tax evasion associated with informal sector consumption. This chapter shows how VAT revenues are affected by increases in the percentage of people in the formal banking system in Argentina, Brazil and Chile from 2002 to 2015. We find that the percentage of people in the banking system is correlated with the rapid rise in the use of credit cards and debit cards in these three middle-income countries. Consequently, more people are using electronic payments (and less cash) for a greater percentage of their daily consumption, a trend observed during the commodity boom but one that continues today.[3] We test two general hypotheses. First, the higher the percentage of the population with bank accounts results in a higher VAT-to-GDP. Second, the increased use of electronic payments (and decreased use of cash) has led to higher VAT-to-GDP by shifting daily household consumption from informal (hard to tax) markets to formal (easier to tax) markets. Specific to recent elevated VAT collection, households persist in shifting more of their consumption to

[3] Linking cash and informal market activities is common in the literature. A good place to start is Rogoff's book *The Curse of Cash* (2016) which argues that record amounts of cash globally feed tax evasion and underground economic activities. As Gordon and Li (2009: 856) state, "...firms can avoid tax payments in any country by shifting entirely to cash transactions and not using the financial sector, thereby avoiding leaving any paper trail. When firms make use of the financial sector, in contrast, the government can gain access to their bank records and use this information in enforcing the tax law. Firms then have to choose whether the economic benefits from use of the financial sector are greater or less than the resulting tax liabilities." Also see Kearney and Schneider (2009), Loayza (1996), and de Soto (1989). See Sung et al. (2017) on South Korea's efforts since 1999 to use credit and debit cards to lower informal sector transactions.

cards, as their overall consumption stagnates or drops—due to safety concerns, ease of use, credit card float in an inflationary context (e.g., Argentina), VAT rebates tied to cards (provided by retailers, banks and governments[4]) and card-based retailer and bank loyalty schemes that proliferated during the commodity boom. The card phenomena result precisely at the stage in national VAT systems observed to be the weakest link in the chain—*final consumption* (Kearney and Schneider 2009; Sung et al. 2017). At earlier stages, producers exchange VAT receipts to the government for tax rebates for their inputs; however, at the stage of final consumption, compliance incentives weaken because neither retailors nor consumers receive a benefit. The threat of an audit lacks the potency of a tax rebate as far as enticing retailers to follow tax law. Using fixed-effects regression for Argentina, Brazil and Chile from 2002 to 2015, we find that the percentage of people with a bank account is positively correlated at a significant level with VAT-to-GDP. Since people generally need a bank account before obtaining a credit card or a debit card, a rising banked population is a necessary condition for an increase in credit card and debit card access and (eventually) use. Consequently, we find a strong positive correlation between the percentage of people with cards and those with bank accounts. As a result, we test the relationship between the use of credit cards, debit cards and cash on VAT-to-GDP in Argentina, Brazil and Chile.

Formal and Informal Banking in South America

Having a formal bank account is important for households because it provides security, consistency, often better savings habits and a path to wealth creation (e.g., buying a home). Rutherford in *The Poor and Their Money* (2000) stresses that there exists throughout the world, however, a chasm between formal banking and banking among low-income households. The primary reason for this is that low-income customers are not cost effective for banks (the margins are too small). As a

[4]Argentina granted a 5% VAT discount on debit card purchases in 2001 and added a 3% VAT discount on credit card purchases in 2003. Argentine officials rescinded the credit card discount in 2009 on equity grounds given that middle- and upper-class people more often used credit cards, and later, in 2017, the government ended debit card VAT discounts. In Argentina, as discussed in Chapter 2, initial VAT discounts helped to cultivate new consumer norms and behavior because without the discounts, consumers continue to use cards.

result, these poorer households find informal ways to save that are inefficient, expensive and sometimes exploitative. But contrary to what some might think, low-income households do save and want to save in efficient ways (see Rutherford 2000). Many low-income people even save for major expenses, such as weddings and funerals. These types of savings take a long time—little by little—and the current informal market is precarious. Hoarding cash around the home or burying it outside not only increases the risk of the money getting stolen or lost, but in South America where inflation is in the solid double digits that cash hoarding is costing households lots of money. This is one reason people convert their pesos and reals into dollars since it is a better store of value. This makes the saving problem even worse, because now someone has dollars that they cannot put into the formal banking system even if they have a bank account. And they do not want to give up the safety and security of having dollars. It also becomes a habit that having dollars feels better psychologically than pesos in a bank account—so that habit must be broken somehow. But the key to helping to reduce the hoarding of dollars is to improve financial inclusion among poorer households—gaining the trust of poorer households and showing how they can save/spend more efficiently and cost effectively.

One response to this problem is microcredit (as shown in Chapter 1), which filled a void in poorer people having no access to credit (especially women in rural villages)—largely because they do not have formal bank accounts (for financial and cultural reasons). As shown in Chapter 1, microcredit started as an egalitarian vision to give poor people the means to lift themselves out of poverty, but this vision has since proved more predatory and malevolent than progressive and benevolent. It was also naïve to think that all poor women in rural Bangladesh need is a little money (at 20% interest!), some social support and a few rules and they could magically become middle-class. Even before the predatory microcredit banks, the results from the Grameen Bank and other microlending organizations were not exceptional. Microcredit might help in the short run, but in the long run, most borrowers fell back into abject poverty or were worse off. As discussed in Chapter 1, many parts of the world that adopted large microcredit schemes had no impact on poverty nor meaningful financial inclusion, such as inculcating greater proportions of people into the formal banking system. The empirical evidence against microcredit's effectiveness is overwhelming. So, does this mean that there is no hope to improve financial inclusion? Not at all.

State assistance is the modus operandi of modern banking. For example, in the United States, there is the Federal Deposit Insurance Corporation (FDIC) created in 1933 after the bank runs in the United States led to thousands of bank failures. As a response to this crisis, the FDIC was created to insure all personal bank deposits (up to $350,000 for a married couple) in cases of bank failure. Also, the Federal Reserve Bank (quasi-government) regulates banks and makes sure that banking services are offered throughout the United States, which is an important part of the original Federal Reserve Act of 1913. Yet, when it comes to helping poorer households to get access to the formal banking system, state interventions are often considered over-reaching. However, the state is in the best position to encourage bank participation among people. This state assistance is particularly important in South America where countries' currencies are prone to crisis (e.g., Argentina, Brazil, Ecuador and Venezuela). People with bank accounts can help stabilize the domestic currency if they are encouraged (incentivized) to keep their money in the domestic formal banking system—increasing demand for the local currency. It is particularly beneficial if people have access to debit cards (and maybe credit cards) that allow them to spend with greater convenience and security, which further strengthens the use of the domestic currency.

There are many benefits to people being in the formal banking system—both microeconomic (e.g., security and convenience) and macroeconomic (e.g., currency stabilization and reducing informal financial markets). As seen in the previous chapter, there is also a strong public finance component to higher bank participation rates. Since VAT (and also sales taxes in Brazil) is the largest source of tax revenue in Argentina, Brazil and Chile, anything that encourages spending in formal markets will help support VAT compliance. However, in the case of poorer households, VAT excludes many household necessities and the poor are able to bypass many of these taxes. Having and using bank accounts do not mean subjecting poor people to a regressive tax. Rather, it is important that taxes are low (or zero) to encourage financial inclusion among poorer households in South America, which is why the state is needed to direct Conditional Cash Transfer (CCT) payments into direct deposit and build trust among people that banks are a safe place to keep their money. This is a public–private partnership where banks get more customers (with no profit) and the state helps to legitimize the banking system by funneling paychecks through it. As the poor get more comfortable saving in banks, the hope is that they will have access to more financial products such as insurance. The idea is not to substitute one predatory lender for another. Rather, the state should keep watch to ensure that banks operate in a way that encourages greater financial inclusion at low costs to customers. Take Argentina as an example of this—the neoliberal era of banking produced dismal financial inclusion results and led to increased informal markets. Comparatively, the public–private partnership throughout the 2000s led to historically high financial inclusion. There is still room to improve, but the major gains in recent years show that with the right public policy nudge, more people will embrace the banking system.

Bank Participation Rates and Electronic Payments

Euromonitor International (2017) provides data on personal finance (e.g., bank accounts, credit cards and debit cards) in South America. From 2002 to 2015, the percentage of the population with a bank account has increased significantly in Argentina (83%), Brazil (36%) and Chile (154%). And during the same period, the number of credit cards owned increased 690% in Argentina, 244% in Brazil and 761% in Chile. Debit card ownership increased over this period by 297% in Argentina, 183% in Brazil and 597% in Chile. Electronic infrastructure grew as well. ATM machines per 100,000 adults increased in Argentina from 21 (2004) to 61 (2015), in Brazil from 104 (2004) to 114 (2015) and in Chile from 33 (2004) to 56 (2015) (World Bank 2017).

Yet, VAT revenue follows card use. After adjusting for inflation, the amount *spent* on credit cards increased in Argentina by 831%, in Brazil by 237% and in Chile by 1131%. Table 3.1 shows card and cash consumption around the height of the commodity boom (2007) and six years after the collapse of commodity prices (2016). Credit cards as a percentage of total consumption increased in all three countries (it more than doubled in Chile), and for debit cards in Argentina and Chile. Brazil's debit card decline is likely explained by its robust card penetration at the start of the commodity boom (2002), compared to Argentina and Chile, and in the context of rapid economic growth after 2002, Brazilian consumers switched from using cards as a mode of exchange (debit cards) toward using them as consumer credit (credit cards). Brazil's overall credit card expenditure gains outpaced debit card declines after 2002. Personal consumer credit research shows that as consumers

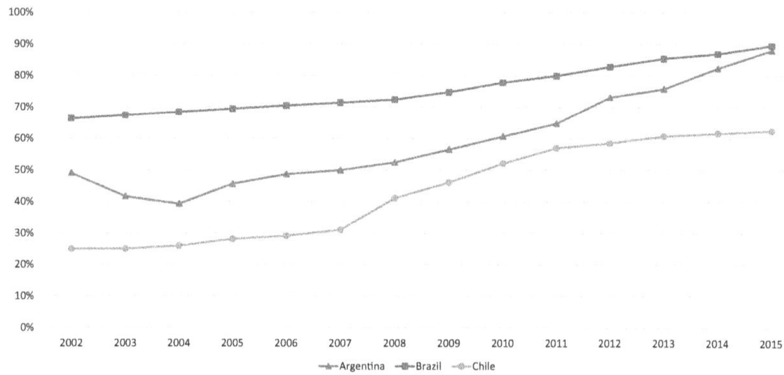

Fig. 3.2 Banked population in Argentina, Brazil and Chile, 2002–2015 (*Source* Authors' calculations using Euromonitor International [2017] data)

enter the formal banking system, their access to credit increases (see Rona-Tas and Guseva 2014). Meanwhile, cash usage decreased in all three countries (notably in Chile). According to research by Stephane Straub (2005), increased cash use is correlated with a larger informal market. Since cash is critical to informal markets, it is not surprising that as the informal market shrank, the use of cash would also decrease.

Figure 3.2 shows a cross-national comparison of the banked population. Brazil starting off with a higher banked population meant its subsequent card-based expenditure lags in terms of growth compared to Argentina and Chile (i.e., Table 3.1). Argentina's banked population dropped to 40% (2004) in the wake of its 2001–2002 sovereign default and economic collapse; however, by 2015, its banked population almost hit an incredible 90%. Chile, lacking the economic turmoil of Argentina, started below 30% yet climbed above 60%. It is interesting that the most deregulated personal finance market, Chile, started our period with the lowest bank participation rate. In sum, a significant percentage of the population entered the formal banking system in the context of the regional commodity boom. What factors encouraged this result?

Often it is assumed that economic growth and its positive consequences (falling poverty, falling unemployment and more disposable income) cause households to enter the bank system. But this is incomplete and discounts the role of public policy. Brazil, as it did with the adoption of VAT, served as an early regional innovator. Its anti-poverty

Table 3.1 Methods of payment (credit cards, debit cards and cash) as a percentage of total personal consumption in Argentina, Brazil and Chile (comparing 2007–2015)

	Credit cards/ consumption		*% change*	*Debit cards/ consumption*		*% change*	*Cash/ consumption*		*% change*
	2007	*2015*		*2007*	*2015*		*2007*	*2015*	
Argentina (%)	46	52.8	+14.8	2.5	2.9	+16	48	44.3	−7.7
Brazil (%)	43.6	47.1	+8.0	24	21	−12.8	29	24.2	−16.6
Chile (%)	15	38.8	+159	29	37.4	+29	56	23.9	−57.3

Source Authors' calculations using Euromonitor International (2017). Credit, Debit and Cash do not sum to 100 in Argentina and Brazil because a small percentage of consumers use travelers checks, store cards, etc., that we exclude

CCT programs date back to the late 1990s, and by 2002, such programs covered millions of households. Today, *Bolsa Familia* alone covers around 14 million households in addition to other CCT-styled programs (*Salário Familia* and *Brasil Carinhoso*, the latter started in 2012). In Brazil, monthly CCT checks are automatically deposited into a bank account. Moreover, Brazil automatically deposits public pension checks and public employee checks.

Argentina's embrace of automatic deposit for public sector transfers gained momentum after the 2001–2002 crisis. Its sovereign default (December 2001) meant exile from international credit markets and an urgent need to find alternative finance for the domestic financial system (i.e., banks). Quickly, the government enforced an existing law requiring automatic deposit of all public payrolls (paychecks and pension checks), it designed a jobs support social program with automatic deposit, and later, it designed CCT programs (Universal Child Allowance in 2009) and a new informal sector pension program (launched in 2012, Argentina now has the largest pension coverage in region at 90%) that all featured automatic deposit to bank accounts (i.e., no cash or checks in the mail or standing in lines outside of government agencies). Argentine banks flush with new clients devised new schemes to encourage use of their personal financial products (i.e., cards)—for example, banks arranged deals with retailers to provide VAT discounts tied to cards. Similar to Argentina, CCT programs in Chile (*Chile Solidario* launched in 2002 and the far more ambitious Ethical Family Income program launched in 2012) and other social programs in recent years use automatic deposit.

The unprecedented increases in the banked population (Fig. 3.2) and consumption via cards (Table 3.1) raise potential concerns. Debit cards are a mere mode of exchange (but are a rough proxy for bank accounts, since there is usually one debit card per bank account), but credit cards amount to the extension of bank credit. High levels of credit card defaults would mean associated advantages as far as more VAT revenue would be one-off—and perhaps more damaging if credit card defaults caused a contraction of future consumer credit from banks. Financial boom and bust cycles are common in the region, so did rapid expansion of card-based consumption in the context of a commodity boom invite reckless consumption? Is this another example of boom followed by bust? Credit cards, of course, can be abused.

The answer is unexpected and requires explanation. The World Bank's data on "bank nonperforming loans to total gross loans" (Fig. 3.3) are an imprecise indicator, but they do include credit cards, and the amount of credit card expenditure listed above means it is a significant percentage of total bank lending. In Argentina, for example, credit card lending is the largest category of total bank consumer loans—credit cards are

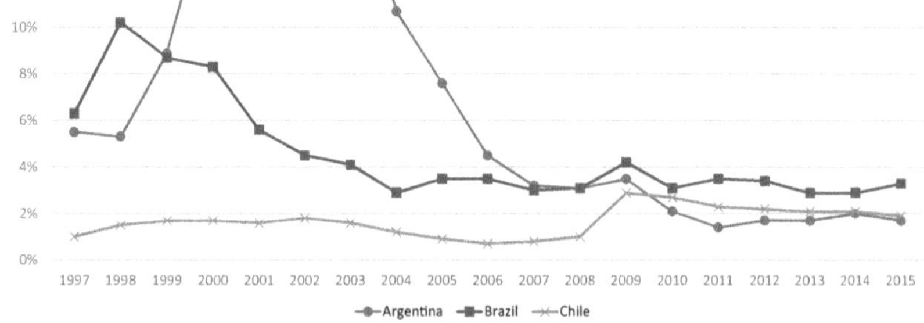

Fig. 3.3 Bank nonperforming loans to total gross loans (*Source* Euromonitor International from World Bank [2017])

31% while mortgages are 17%.[5] To add some comparative context, for the year 2016, the same World Bank dataset lists the USA at 1.3%, Spain at 5.6%, Italy at 17.1%, Greece 36.3%, the OECD average at 2.7% and the world upper middle-income country average at 4.9%. This means Argentina (1.8%) and Chile (1.8%), our two case studies in which credit card use increased the most, outperformed the OECD average in 2016. Interestingly, Argentina and Chile have been stuck between stagnation and recession since 2011 but on nonperforming bank loans, they outperform the OECD. And Brazil (3.9%), mired in a deep recession, outperformed the global middle-income country average.

The take away is that the shift by consumers into cards and away from cash did not lead to reckless, unsustainable consumer behavior (i.e., credit card defaults) that might contribute to a more general economic bust. Recent adverse macroeconomic performance (stagnant GDP growth, lower household consumption, rising unemployment, etc.) in Argentina, Brazil and Chile has not been caused by reckless consumer behavior (as say occurred in the United States, United Kingdom and Spain prior to 2008). Also, despite an adverse macroeconomic environment, consumers continue to shift into cards.

Financial Inclusion

The Global Findex dataset is “the world’s most comprehensive dataset on how adults save, borrow, make payments and manage risk” (The World Bank 2018a). The surveys are distributed to over 150,000 people across more than 140 countries. The Bill & Melinda Gates Foundation provides the funding for Findex. The data are collected triennially from surveys distributed to households by Gallup, Inc. There are currently three waves of data (2011, 2014 and 2017) available for analysis. All the questions asked in the 2011 survey are in following surveys; however, more questions were added to the 2014 (and 2017) surveys. The purpose of Findex is to gauge how well countries are doing with regard to financial access. The World Bank has a goal of universal financial access by 2020. The central goals of this initiative are (a) “that by 2020, adults, who currently aren’t part of the formal financial system, are able to have access

[5] Similarly, Argentina’s non-performing consumer loans (>90-days delinquent in repayment) which includes credit cards decreased from 9.1% in 2004 to 2.9% in 2013—as a percentage of all other bank loans.

to a transaction account to store money, send and receive payments as the basic building block to manage their financial lives" and (b) "enabling 1 billion people to gain access to a transaction account through targeted interventions" [read: mobile phones] (The World Bank 2018b).

The idea is for people with mobile phones to be able to deposit, access, send and receive money electronically. This initiative is perfectly fine, in general, and may even prove valuable for all people regardless of their financial status; but why is this an important goal for poor households? The World Bank even states "Globally, 59% of adults without an account cite a lack of enough money as a key reason, which implies that financial services aren't yet affordable or designed to fit low income (sic) users" (The World Bank 2018b). Or maybe these households are too poor to buy basic necessities and having access to a bank account is irrelevant.

In Table 3.2, we see that a lack of money is the primary reason people do not have bank accounts. Cost is the second most predominant factor, but that could be tied to a lack of money, in general. Thinking in terms of "use" rather than simply having an account, once someone has a credit card, they are highly likely to use that card. The same is also true of debit cards, but not to the same extent as credit cards. Credit cards have several important advantages: buy now and paying later lets people take advantage of the float, which is particularly advantageous in countries with high inflation (money tomorrow is worth less than money today). Also, credit cards offer more buyer protections than credit cards, in general.

Tables 3.3, 3.4, and 3.5 show the change in bank account ownership and credit card and debit card ownership based on whether someone is in the low-income group (less than 40th income percentile), middle-income group (between 40th and 80th income percentile) and high-income group (above the 80th income percentile). Gains in accounts, card ownership and savings transpired between 2011 and 2017, a period of poor macroeconomic performance in all three countries and steep economic decline in Brazil. Interestingly, Argentina and Brazil experienced major economic contractions from 2014 to 2017, but among low-income households, account ownership and savings climbed. Rutherford's view of the poor and their money maintains that the non-banked poor "save" money (usually in tin cans or under a mattress) and if permitted to access to the formal banking system, this population would continue to save.

Table 3.2 Financial inclusion in Argentina, Brazil and Chile, 2011–2017

	Argentina			*Brazil*			*Chile*		
	2011 (%)	*2014 (%)*	*2017 (%)*	*2011 (%)*	*2014 (%)*	*2017 (%)*	*2011 (%)*	*2014 (%)*	*2017 (%)*
Has bank account	33.1	50.2	47.9	56.1	68.1	70.0	42.2	63.3	74.3
Why no account?									
Too expensive	37.6	21.8	44.8	45.9	22.8	57.8	47.4	46.4	55.7
Lack documents	20.5	26.8	30.6	26.3	10.7	19.1	23.4	16.2	23.4
Do not trust banks	27.5	20.0	26.1	21.0	8.3	25.6	38.4	43.6	45.4
No money	63.3	45.0	60.0	64.8	65.3	58.2	67.1	47.5	57.6
Has debit card (DC)	29.9	44.3	41.6	41.4	59.3	59.6	25.8	54.2	60.1
Used DC last year	*	58.1	55.0	*	70.4	57.5	*	75.8	80.1
Has credit card (CC)	22.0	26.6	24.3	29.5	32.2	27.1	22.9	28.2	30.0
Used CC last year		90.00	87.70		88.70	83.70		80.80	83.30
Saved last year	24.70	23.10	30.30	21.20	28.00	33.00	27.20	36.00	49.20

Source The World Bank (2018a)

Table 3.3 Account ownership based on income level for Argentina, Brazil and Chile, 2011

	Argentina			*Brazil*			*Chile*		
	Low	*Middle*	*High*	*Low*	*Middle*	*High*	*Low*	*Middle*	*High*
Account (%)	19.2	36.0	56.2	39.6	61.2	78.6	29.6	43.0	66.8
Debit card (%)	16.2	33.3	51.4	25.1	45.1	66.5	14.5	25.3	50.1
Credit card (%)	8.8	26.1	40.7	15.3	31.6	52.9	14.0	22.1	43.1
Saved last year (%)	15.8	24.3	44.7	17.1	22.3	27.4	19.4	27.8	41.9

Source The World Bank (2018a)

Table 3.4 Account ownership based on income level for Argentina, Brazil and Chile, 2014

	Argentina			*Brazil*			*Chile*		
	Low	*Middle*	*High*	*Low*	*Middle*	*High*	*Low*	*Middle*	*High*
Account (%)	39.7	53.2	64.9	58.5	70.0	84.1	56.4	64.8	73.9
Debit card (%)	36.8	43.3	61.1	42.9	65.1	81.2	45.4	56.2	67.6
Credit card (%)	15.4	31.0	40.4	19.7	34.0	54.5	21.0	27.1	44.7
Saved last year (%)	16.3	23.3	36.3	18.6	27.9	47.3	26.2	38.1	51.1

Source The World Bank (2018a)

Table 3.5 Account ownership based on income level for Argentina, Brazil and Chile, 2017

	Argentina			*Brazil*			*Chile*		
	Low	*Middle*	*High*	*Low*	*Middle*	*High*	*Low*	*Middle*	*High*
Account (%)	37.4	50.0	64.6	56.6	74.4	88.0	66.9	75.2	87.5
Debit card (%)	28.7	44.6	61.6	44.2	63.6	82.0	52.1	58.6	78.8
Credit card (%)	14.4	23.7	44.9	15.6	26.3	45.7	21.1	27.6	52.4
Saved last year (%)	21.2	33.1	42.8	25.2	32.4	47.2	40.4	47.0	71.0

Source The World Bank (2018a)

Methodology

We estimate seven econometric models using panel data for Argentina, Brazil and Chile. We have balanced panel datasets that control for heterogeneity among countries and use fixed-effects regression to control for serial correlation. Hausman tests determined fixed-effects was the correct estimation method in all cases (no stationary variables are used). Our first three models use data from 2002 to 2015. Our last four models use data from 2007 to 2015—because 2007 was the earliest data available for our independent variables of interest. We estimate the following panel data model:

$$y_{it} = \alpha_i + X_{it}\beta + \gamma_t + U_{it},$$

where y_{it} is Value-Added Tax Revenue-to-Gross Domestic Product (VAT/GDP) for all models. To explain the VAT revenue-to-GDP, the following X_{it} explanatory variables are included, which are identified by earlier literature (Aizenman and Jinjarak 2005; Cukierman et al. 1992) as factors influencing VAT (included in all models):

- Natural log of GDP per capita
- Gini coefficient
- Percent of GDP from agriculture
- Percent of GDP from imports
- Index of economic freedom
- Dummy variables for all years.

New variables of interest in our study (years 2002–2015):

- Percentage of the population (15+ years of age) with a bank account
- Natural log of the amount spent using credit cards per capita
- Natural log of the percent of the economy that is informal.

New variables of interest in our study (years 2007–2015):

- Credit card use as a percent of total consumption
- Debit card use as a percent of total consumption
- Combination of credit cards and debit cards as a percent of total consumption
- Cash use as a percent of total consumption.

Hypotheses

Based on the above analysis, we test the following hypotheses:

H1: The higher the percentage of the population with bank accounts results in higher VAT/GDP and a lower informal sector.
$H1_a$: Higher percentages of people with bank accounts leads to higher VAT/GDP.
$H1_b$: As the amount spent using credit cards per person increases, VAT/GDP will rise.
$H1_c$: As the informal market shrinks as a percentage of the total economy, VAT/GDP increases.

H2: The increased use of electronic payments has led to higher VAT/GDP.
$H2_a$: As credit cards are used for a greater percentage of payments, VAT/GDP will increase.
$H2_b$: As debit cards are used for a greater percentage of payments, VAT/GDP will increase.
$H2_c$: The use of electronic payments (measured as a combination of credit cards and debit cards) is positively correlated with VAT/GDP.
$H2_d$: Cash used as a percentage of payments is negatively correlated with VAT/GDP.

Table 3.6 shows the descriptive statistics from 2002 to 2015. Argentina, Brazil and Chile are similar across many measures—though differences exist in imports/GDP and agriculture/GDP.

Results

Table 3.7 includes the fixed-effects regression results testing our *H1* hypotheses. We find that the banked population percentage ($H1_a$) is positively correlated with VAT-to-GDP. For each one percent increase in the banked population, VAT-to-GDP rises 0.05%. The amount spent using credit cards per capita ($H1_b$) is positively correlated with VAT-to-GDP. Also, the informal economy is inversely related to VAT-to-GDP, so as the informal market shrinks by shifting more consumption into the formal market, then VAT-to-GDP grows. Specifically, a one-percent increase in VAT-to-GDP is correlated with a 10.63% relative decrease in the informal market (e.g., from 20% down to 17.87%).

Table 3.6 Descriptive statistics from 2002–2015 for Argentina, Brazil and Chile

	Median	*Mean*	*Std. Dev.*	*Minimum*	*Maximum*
Argentina					
VAT/GDP	7.0%	6.7%	0.9	4.5%	7.4%
Banked population	54.5%	59.1%	15.5	39.2%	88.1%
Informal economy	22.3%	22.9%	1.7	20.8%	26.2%
Gini	42.2	42.4	3.4	38.2	48.6
Agriculture/GDP	8.4%	8.4%	1.5	6.0%	11.0%
Imports/GDP	15.3%	15.6%	1.9	11.9%	18.3%
GDP-per-capita	$8557	$8578	$3923	$2579	$13,467
Freedom index	52.0	52.0	5.4	44.1	65.7
Card transactions/pop'	13.3	13.4	5.4	5.5	23.2
Cards-per-population	1.1	1.2	0.5	0.4	2.1
Brazil					
VAT/GDP	7.6%	7.7%	0.4	7.2%	8.4%
Banked population	73.6%	75.9%	7.8	66.3%	89.6%
Informal economy	36.1%	35.8%	2.3	32.6%	38.9%
Gini	51.2	51.9	2.1	50.0	56.3
Agriculture/GDP	5.2%	5.5%	0.7	4.8%	7.2%
Imports/GDP	13.0%	12.8%	1.0	11.3%	14.1%
GDP-per-capita	$8655	$8177	$3684	$2820	$13,167
Freedom index	57.3	58.5	2.7	55.6	63.4
Card transactions/pop'	13.7	14.8	8.1	4.5	28.0
Cards-per-population	1.8	1.7	0.5	0.8	2.2
Chile					
VAT/GDP	7.9%	7.9%	0.4	7.0%	8.4%
Banked population	43.6%	43.2%	15.4	25.0%	62.5%
Informal economy	14.3%	14.8%	1.9	12.6%	18.3%
Gini	39.8	39.9	1.0	38.6	41.6
Agriculture/GDP	3.7%	4.0%	0.7	3.2%	5.5%
Imports/GDP	31.6%	32.2%	2.7	29.5%	39.5%
GDP-per-capita	$10,654	$10,823	$3935	$4464	$15,941
Freedom index	77.9	77.9	0.8	76.0	79.0
Card transactions/pop'	11.3	11.7	7.4	2.5	24.0
Cards-per-population	1.9	1.5	0.8	0.4	2.4

Source Authors' calculations using data from Euromonitor International (2017). All dollar figures are in 2015 United States Dollars

Table 3.8 shows our results from fixed-effects regressions testing our *H2* hypotheses. First, we find that a higher percentage of payments made using credit cards ($H2_a$) leads to a higher VAT-to-GDP. For each one percent increase in credit cards as the method of payment results

Table 3.7 Fixed-effects regression results for percent of banked population and credit card spending per capita, 2002–2015

	Percent of banked population	*Credit card spending per capita*	*Informal economy*
Intercept	24.95	29.43	67.06***
	(22.17)	(19.45)	(16.94)
Banked	0.05*		
	(0.03)		
lnCCpop		1.16**	
		(0.46)	
LnInformal			−10.63***
			(2.98)
lnGDPc	−1.32	−2.07	−1.43
	(1.85)	(1.59)	(1.46)
Gini coefficient	−0.25**	−0.24**	−0.32***
	(0.10)	(0.10)	(0.09)
Agriculture	−0.26	−0.29	−0.65***
	(0.22)	(0.19)	(0.16)
Imports	0.12	0.09	−0.02
	(0.08)	(0.07)	(.06)
Economic freedom index	−0.01	−0.04	−0.03
	(0.05)	(0.05)	(0.04)
R-squared	0.83	0.81	0.86

Source Authors' calculations using data from Euromonitor International (2017). Standard errors in parenthesis. ***significant at 1%; **significant at 5% and *significant at 10%

in a 0.06% increase in VAT-to-GDP. Likewise, debit card use ($H2_b$) is also positively correlated with VAT-to-GDP, such that a one percent increase in debit card use translated into a 0.1% increase in VAT-to-GDP. Consequently, combining debit cards and credit cards ($H2_c$) showed a positive correlation with VAT-to-GDP. Lastly, as expected, higher percentages of cash used as the method of payment ($H2_d$) are negatively correlated with VAT-to-GDP. A one percent increase in the use of cash as the method of payment *reduces* VAT-to-GDP by 0.05%.

Comparing the regression results in Table 3.8 with the method of payment data in Table 3.1, we can see that between 2007 and 2015, significant changes occurred in the preference for electronic payments over cash—and these changes had a cumulative and dramatic impact on VAT-to-GDP in these countries. One might expect that substituting cash with cards would not result in more tax collection since the method

Table 3.8 Fixed-effects regression results for methods of payment, 2007–2015

	Credit cards	*Debit cards*	*Credit and debit*	*Cash*
Intercept	26.47	−8.12	33.67**	19.01
	(7.17)	(11.66)	(12.83)	(7.09)
Credit cards	0.06***			
	(0.01)			
Debit cards		0.10***		
		(0.03)		
Credit and debit cards			0.06***	
			(0.02)	
Cash				−0.05***
				(0.01)
lnGDPc	−1.10	1.27	−1.84	−0.13
	(0.61)	(0.98)	(1.09)	(0.60)
Gini coefficient	−0.27***	0.08	−0.31**	−0.17**
	(0.06)	(0.08)	(0.11)	(0.05)
Agriculture	−0.10	−0.06	−0.20	−0.07
	(0.07)	(0.11)	(0.12)	(0.07)
Imports	0.02	0.05	−0.03	0.03
	(0.03)	(0.04)	(0.04)	(0.03)
Economic freedom index	0.00	−0.05	0.03	−0.03
	(0.02)	(0.04)	(0.04)	(0.02)
R-squared	0.96	0.90	0.90	0.96

Source Authors' calculations use data from Euromonitor International (2017). Standard errors in parenthesis. ***significant at 1%; **significant at 5% and *significant at 10%

of payment does not change overall consumption; however, in Latin America, the large informal sector of the economy is able to bypass VAT and other taxes by relying on cash. Once more people start using cards (e.g., because of convenience, security or shifting consumer cultural norms), they are more likely to shop in the formal market (perhaps even unaware that they are doing so).

Conclusion

Due to successful government efforts in the area of financial inclusion, Argentina, Brazil and Chile from 2002 to 20015 recorded sizable increases in the percentage of people with a bank account (especially Argentina and Chile). Simultaneously, and more importantly, the issuance and use of credit cards and debit cards grew at a rapid pace in

Argentina and Chile (and credit cards in Brazil). Our findings above suggest that the increased use of electronic payments and lower usage of cash are likely shifting some consumption from informal (hard to tax) markets to formal (easier to tax) markets, leading to more VAT revenue. Multilateral and academic VAT evasion research points to final consumption (i.e., transactions between retailers and consumers) as the critical underperforming area in national VAT systems and it is here that rising card ownership and card use have mattered the most. Consumer preference for cards over cash continues to the present day, thus we anticipate a scenario (and found one in this analysis) in which it is possible for the same quantity of expenditure (say on food, the largest item in household consumption) can produce more VAT revenue (and sales taxes in Brazil). This chapter demonstrates empirically how this is possible (Tables 3.7 and 3.8). VAT revenue across these countries has grown (Argentina and Chile) or remained stable (Brazil) after the commodity boom ended (as shown in Table 3.1). Macroeconomic stagnation after 2009 should have (and was expected to result) resulted in lower VAT yields given past experiences in the 1990s—but the opposite has occurred.

Public policy, more than market forces, impacts the population with bank accounts in our case studies. Chile's experience is illustrative. In 2002, its personal finance market was more deregulated, and its macroeconomic performance more positive and stable; yet, it produced a significantly lower bank participation rate than Brazil and Argentina, a situation that began to turn around after Chile started following the examples of Brazil and Argentina. Moving more people into the banking system serves as a critical first step in reducing cash-based consumption and recent government schemes utilizing automatic deposit (social policy, pensions and public payrolls) are pivotal and should be amplified. Banks in Argentina, Brazil and Chile responded to the opportunity presented to them in the form of new clients by offering attractive personal finance services. VAT rebates tied to cards and regular daily expenditure are an area that governments should explore more because it can be attractive to *retailers* (who want consumers), to *consumers* (who want lower prices), to *banks* (who want clients, both consumers and retailers) and to *governments* (that desire less cash expenditures and more VAT revenue). Related, consumption is the largest component of GDP in our case studies. Size matters. The positive impact on VAT-to-GDP associated with card expenditure and the negative impact on VAT-to-GDP of cash expenditure may appear small, but placed in the context of overall consumption, such differences become significant.

References

Aizenman, J., Jinjarak, Y. 2005. "The Collection Efficiency of the Value Added Tax: Theory and International Experience." Working Paper 11539.

Artana, D., and I. Templado. 2010. *Is the Argentine Revenue Effort "too" High?*. Fundación de Investigaciones Económicas Latinoamericanas.

Azaria, N. T., and Z. Robinson. 2005. "The Revenue Raising Capabilities of a VAT System in Developing Countries: Economics." *South African Journal of Economic and Management Sciences* 8 (1): 63–76.

Bergman, M. S. 2003. "Tax Reforms and Tax Compliance: The Divergent Paths of Chile and Argentina." *Journal of Latin American Studies* 35 (3): 593–624.

Bergman, M., and A. Nevarez. 2006. "Do Audits Enhance Compliance? An Empirical Assessment of VAT Enforcement." *National Tax Journal* 817–832.

Bird, R. M., and P. P. Gendron. 2007. *The VAT in Developing and Transitional Countries*. Cambridge, Cambridge University Press.

Bird, R. M., and E. M. Zolt. 2015. "Fiscal Contracting in Latin America." *World Development* 67: 323–335.

CEPAL. 2016. Fiscal Panorama of Latin America and the Caribbean 2016: Public Finances and the Challenge of Reconciling Austerity with Growth and Equality. Washington, DC: CEPAL.

Cnossen, S. 1998. "Global Trends and Issues in Value Added Taxation." *International Tax and Public Finance* 5: 399–428.

Cukierman, A., S. Edwards, and G. Tabellini. 1992. "Seigniorage and Political Instability." *American Economic Review* 82: 537–555.

De Soto, H. 1989. *The Other Path*. New York: Harper & Row.

Due, J. F. 1974. "The Value Added Tax-Sense and Nonsense." *Nebraska Journal of Economics and Business* 13 (4): 54–65.

Ebrill, L. P., ed. 2001. *The Modern VAT*. Washington, DC: International Monetary Fund.

Euromonitor International. 2017. Consumer Expenditures. Retrieved from Euromonitor Passport Database.

Focanti, D., M. Hallerberg, and C. Scartascini. 2016. "Tax Reforms in Latin America in an Era of Democracy." *Latin American Research Review* 51 (1): 132–158.

Gomez-Sabaini, J. C., and D. Moran. 2014. Tax Policy in Latin America. Macroeconomics of development series 133. Santiago: ECLAC.

Gordon, R., and W. Li. 2009. "Tax Structures in Developing Countries: Many puzzles and a Possible Explanation." *Journal of Public Economics* 93: 855–866.

Hallerberg, M., and C. Scartascini. 2016. "Explaining Changes in Tax Burdens in Latin America: Do Politics Trump Economics?" *European Journal of Political Economy* 48: 162–179.

Kearney, A. T., and F. Schneider. 2009. "The Shadow Economy in Europe: Using Payment Systems to Combat the Shadow Economy." A. T. Kearney. https://www.atkearney.com/documents/10192/1f89864d-903f-4683-b6e4-df57e223a4d7.

Keen, M., and J. Mintz. 2004. "The Optimal Threshold for a Value-Added Tax." *Journal of Public Economics* 88 (3): 559–576.

Lindholm, R. 1974. "The Value Added Tax: A Short Review of the Literature." *Journal of Economic Literature* 8 (4): 1178–1189.

Loayza, N. 1996. The Economics of the Informal Sector: A Simple Model and Some Empirical Evidence from Latin America. *Carnegie-Rochester Conference Series on Public Policy* 45: 129–162.

Lustig, N., and D. McLeod. 2009. *Are Latin America's New Left Regimes Reducing Inequality Faster?* Washington, DC, Woodrow Wilson Center for International Scholars, Latin American Program. Washington, DC: Wilson Center.

Mahon, J. 2004. "Causes of Tax Reform in Latin America, 1977–1995." *Latin American Research Review* 39 (1): 3–30.

Mahon, J. 2012. *Tax Incidence and Tax Reforms in Latin America*. Woodrow Wilson Center Update on the Americas. Washington, DC: Wilson Center.

Melo, M. A. 2007. "Institutional Weakness and the Puzzle of Argentina's Low Taxation." *Latin American Politics and Society* 49 (4): 115–148.

Mitchell, K., and R. H. Scott. 2018. Will That Be Cash or Credit? Payment Preferences and Rising VAT in Argentina. *Journal of Post Keynesian Economics* Forthcoming.

Rogoff, K. 2016. *The Curse of Cash*. Princeton: Princeton University Press.

Rona-Tas, A., and A. Guseva. 2014. *Plastic Capital: Constructing Markets for Credit Cards in Eight Postcommunist Countries*. Stanford, CA: Stanford University Press.

Rutherford, Stuart. 2000. *The Poor and Their Money*. Oxford, UK: Oxford University Press.

Sanchez, O. 2011. "Fighting Tax Evasion in Latin America: The Contrasting Strategies of Chile and Argentina." *Third World Quarterly* 32 (6): 1107–1125.

Sanchez Román, J. A. 2012. *Taxation and Society in Twentieth-Century Argentina*. London: Springer.

Spiller, P. T., and M. Tommasi. 2007. *The Institutional Foundations of Public Policy in Argentina*. New York, NY: Cambridge University Press.

Straub, S. 2005. "Informal Sector: The Credit Market Channel." *Journal of Development Economics* 78 (2): 299–321.

Sung, M. J., R. Awasthi, and H. C. Lee. 2017. Can Tax Incentives for Electronic Payments Reduce the Shadow Economy? Korea's Attempt to Reduce Underreporting in Retail Businesses. Policy Research Working Paper 7936, World Bank.

Tanzi, V. 1992. "Fiscal Policy and Economic Reconstruction in Latin America." *World Development* 20 (5): 641–657.

Tanzi, V. 2007. "Argentina: An Economic Chronicle." *How One of the Richest Countries in the World Lost Its Wealth.* New York: Jorge Pinto Books Inc.

The World Bank. 2014. Social Gains in the Balance. A fiscal policy challenge for Latin America and the Caribbean. World Bank Document #85162, World Bank, Washington, DC.

The World Bank. 2018a. Global Findex. https://globalfindex.worldbank.org/.

The World Bank. 2018b. UFA2020 Overview: Universal Financial Access by 2020. http://www.worldbank.org/en/topic/financialinclusion/brief/achieving-universal-financial-access-by-2020.

World Bank. 2017. "DataBank." World Bank. databank.worldbank.org/data/home.aspx.

Conclusion

This book has emphasized that greater and more stable tax collection is possible and necessary for South American countries to provide the services and infrastructure needed to thrive in a challenging global economy. The difference in tax revenue as a percentage of GDP between developed and developing nations stresses this need to generate public revenue. In South America it is also important because the region is prone to financial crises that set the region back economically and create political upheaval and hardship. A principal cause of economic breakdown in the region is a lack of OECD-level and reliable public revenue. Indeed, ECLAC and Oxfam collaborated on a recent study "Time to Tax for Inclusive Growth" (March 2016: 9) that states compliance has increased among Latin American tax payers and more importantly, "[C]hanging consumption patterns, associated with the region's growing middle class, have also served to reduce evasion as purchases are shifted from local markets to big box retailers who are more likely to collect VAT and issue legal receipts."

In Chapters 2 and 3 we explain how VAT revenue in Argentina, Brazil and Chile became the dominant public revenue source. These countries, however, have historically had large informal (shadow) economies that cut into VAT revenue. We showed empirically, however, that significant increases in financial inclusion in the form of bank accounts, credit cards and debit cards is shifting more consumption from informal markets to formal markets. As a result, VAT revenue has increased and stabilized

K. Mitchell and R. H. Scott, III, *Pesos or Plastic?*,
https://doi.org/10.1007/978-3-030-14876-8

(especially in Argentina). These findings provide hope that raising tax revenues does not require major tax overhaul, dictatorial oversight or changing the culture around taxes. Our story suggests that getting more people into and using the banking system encourages formal consumption. And more formal consumption in the future will be the key to more VAT revenue.

In light of the above, we propose that developing countries consider a three-step approach. Step one, at a macro or general policy level, countries should move toward a uniform, single-rate national VAT because it is preferable on efficiency grounds to ad hoc, multi-rate systems with numerous exemptions. Simplicity, as demonstrated in Chile, is the proven path to less VAT evasion and maximizing revenue. Coupled with the shift to a single-rate system, governments must make a strong commitment to earmark new VAT revenues for specific social programs such as education, health and pensions. Europe's experience with VAT attests to the fact that "everyone pays, everyone gains" is a successful approach.

Step two, government must become an active agent for financial inclusion through its interactions with the public. Argentina provides a general blueprint, but more can be done in the future. All public payments (wages, pensions, CCTs, tax rebates, etc.) must be directly deposited into an individual bank account. All revenue paid by people to the state such as public bills (utilities, trash, etc.), fines (parking, insider trading, etc.), and fees (motor vehicle, public transport, tolls, passport/visas, licenses/permits, etc.), must be done through formal bank accounts either by transfers or credit cards. In short, direct deposit and electronic payments must become a new societal norm across the public sector.

Step three, government should encourage cashless transactions, both firm-to-firm and firm-to-final consumer transactions. VAT rebates to consumers for card-use is a place to begin. Similarly, with SMEs, offer corporate income tax rebates on all electronic revenue. Our objective is to alter consumer and retailor norms slowly (something that has already started) rather than advise a dramatic "shock therapy" approach such as ending printed currency. Such a radical change given the reality of limited state capacity is unlikely to produce a desired outcome. Technology advances already permit small venders to accept payments via cellphone. Once state policies encourage more people into the private or public banking system, the banks must accept new regulations on personal banking services and the state must take its regulatory duties seriously. For the banks, new clients via financial inclusion must mean new responsibilities. Initial regulations would include caps on credit card interest rates, caps on fees, and caps on fines. These three steps provide a general strategy to shrink informal economies by lowering evasion and to grow VAT revenues that can be utilized to help countries tackle the economic challenges of the twenty-first century.

Index

K. Mitchell and R. H. Scott, III, *Pesos or Plastic?*,
https://doi.org/10.1007/978-3-030-14876-8

CPSIA information can be obtained
at www.ICGtesting.com
Printed in the USA
LVHW050019020419
612562LV00018B/467/P

9 783030 148751